American Political Ideas Viewed from the Standpoint of Universal History

by John Fiske

I0411745

TO

EDWARD LIVINGSTON YOUMANS

NOBLEST OF MEN AND DEAREST OF FRIENDS

WHOSE UNSELFISH AND UNTIRING WORK IN EDUCATING THE AMERICAN
PEOPLE IN THE PRINCIPLES OF SOUND PHILOSOPHY DESERVES THE
GRATITUDE OF ALL MEN

I dedicate this Book

PREFACE.

In the spring of 1879 I gave at the Old South Meeting-house in Boston a course of lectures on the discovery and colonization of America, and presently, through the kindness of my friend Professor Huxley, the course was repeated at University College in London. The lectures there were attended by very large audiences, and awakened such an interest in American history that I was invited to return to England in the following year and treat of some of the philosophical aspects of my subject in a course of lectures at the Royal Institution.

In the three lectures which were written in response to this invitation, and which are now published in this little volume, I have endeavoured to illustrate some of the fundamental ideas of American politics by setting forth their relations to the general history of mankind. It is impossible thoroughly to grasp the meaning of any group of facts, in any department of study, until we have duly compared them with allied groups of facts; and the political history of the American people can be rightly understood only when it is studied in connection with that general process of political evolution which has been going on from the earliest times, and of which it is itself one of the most important and remarkable phases. The government of the United States is not the result of special creation, but of evolution. As the town-meetings of New England are lineally descended from the village assemblies of the early Aryans; as our huge federal union was long ago foreshadowed in the little leagues of Greek cities and Swiss cantons; so the great political problem which we are (thus far successfully) solving is the very same problem upon which all civilized peoples have been working ever since civilization began. How to insure peaceful concerted action throughout the Whole, without infringing upon local and individual freedom in the Parts,--this has ever been the chief aim of civilization, viewed on its political side; and we rate the failure or success of nations politically according to their failure or success in attaining this supreme end. When thus considered in the light of the comparative method, our American history acquires added dignity and interest, and a broad and rational basis is secured for the detailed treatment of political questions.

When viewed in this light, moreover, not only does American history become especially interesting to Englishmen, but English history is clothed with fresh interest for Americans. Mr. Freeman has done well in insisting upon the fact that the history of the English people does not begin with the Norman Conquest. In the deepest and widest sense, our American history does not begin with the Declaration of Independence, or even with the settlements of Jamestown and Plymouth; but it descends in unbroken continuity from the days when stout Arminius in the forests of northern Germany successfully defied the might of imperial Rome. In a more restricted sense, the statesmanship of Washington and Lincoln appears in the noblest light when regarded as the fruition of the various work of De Montfort and Cromwell and Chatham. The good fight begun at Lewes and continued at Naseby and Quebec was fitly crowned at Yorktown and at Appomattox. When we duly realize this, and further come to see how the two great branches of the English race have the common mission of establishing throughout the larger part of the earth a higher civilization and more permanent political order than any that has gone before, we shall the better understand the true significance of the history which English-speaking men have so magnificently wrought out upon American soil.

In dealing concisely with a subject so vast, only brief hints and suggestions can be expected; and I have not thought it worth while, for the present at least, to change or amplify the manner of treatment. The lectures are printed exactly as they were delivered at the Royal Institution, more than four years ago. On one point of detail some change will very likely by and by be called for. In the lecture on the Town-meeting I have adopted the views of Sir Henry Maine as to the common holding of the arable land in the ancient German mark, and as to the primitive character of the periodical redistribution of land in the Russian village community. It now seems highly probable that these views will have to undergo serious modification in consequence of the valuable evidence lately brought forward by my friend Mr. Denman Ross, in his learned and masterly treatise on "The Early History of Landholding among the Germans;" but as I am not yet quite clear as to how far this modification will go, and as it can in nowise affect the general drift of my argument, I have made no change in my incidental remarks on this difficult and disputed question.

In describing some of the characteristic features of country life in New England, I had especially in mind the beautiful mountain village in which this preface is written, and in which for nearly a quarter of a century I have felt myself more at home than in any other spot in the world.

In writing these lectures, designed as they were for a special occasion, no attempt was made to meet the ordinary requirements of popular audiences; yet they have been received in many places with unlooked-for favour. The lecture on "Manifest Destiny" was three times repeated in London, and once in Edinburgh; seven times in Boston; four times in New York; twice in Brooklyn, N.Y., Plainfield, N.J., and Madison, Wis.; once in Washington, Baltimore, Philadelphia, Buffalo, Cleveland, Cincinnati, Indianapolis, St. Louis, and Milwaukee; in Appleton and Waukesha, Wis.; Portland, Lewiston, and Brunswick, Me.; Lowell, Concord, Newburyport, Peabody, Stoneham, Maiden, Newton Highlands, and Martha's Vineyard, Mass.; Middletown and Stamford, Conn.; Newburg and Poughkeepsie, N.Y.; Orange, N.J.; and at Cornell University and Haverford College. In several of these places the course was given.

PETERSHAM, _September 13, 1884_.

CONTENTS

I.

THE TOWN-MEETING

Differences in outward aspect between a village in England and a village in Massachusetts. Life in a typical New England mountain village. Tenure of land, domestic service, absence of poverty and crime, universality of labour and of culture, freedom of thought, complete democracy. This state of things is to some extent passing away. Remarkable characteristics of the Puritan settlers of New England, and extent to which their characters and aims have influenced American history. Town governments in New England. Different meanings of the word "city" in England and America. Importance of local self-government in the political life of the United States. Origin of the town-meeting. Mr. Freeman on the cantonal assemblies of Switzerland. The old Teutonic "mark," or dwelling-place of a clan. Political union originally based, not on territorial contiguity, but on blood-relationship. Divisions of the mark. Origin of the village Common. The _mark-mote_. Village communities in Russia and Hindustan. Difference between the despotism of Russia and that of France under the Old Regime. Elements of sound political life fostered by the Russian village. Traces of the mark in England. Feudalization of Europe, and partial metamorphosis of the mark or township into the manor. Parallel transformation of the township, in some of its features, into the parish. The court leet and the vestry-meeting. The New England town-meeting a revival of the ancient mark-mote.

Vicissitudes of local self-government in the various portions of the Aryan world illustrated in the contrasted cases of France and England. Significant contrast between the aristocracy of England and that of the Continent. Difference between the Teutonic conquests of Gaul and of Britain. Growth of centralization in France. Why the English have always been more successful than the French in founding colonies. Struggle between France and England for the possession of North America, and prodigious significance of the victory of England.

II.

THE FEDERAL UNION.

Wonderful greatness of ancient Athens. Causes of the political failure of Greek civilization. Early stages of political aggregation,--the hundred, the

[Greek: _phratria_], the _curia_; the shire, the deme, and the pagus. Aggregation of clans into tribes. Differences in the mode of aggregation in Greece and Rome on the one hand, and in Teutonic countries on the other. The Ancient City. Origin of cities in Hindustan, Germany, England, and the United States. Religious character of the ancient city. Burghership not granted to strangers. Consequences of the political difference between the Graeco-Roman city and the Teutonic shire. The _folk-mote_, or primary assembly, and the witenagemote, or assembly of notables. Origin of representative government in the Teutonic shire. Representation unknown to the Greeks and Romans. The ancient city as a school for political training. Intensity of the jealousies and rivalries between adjacent self-governing groups of men. Smallness of simple social aggregates and universality of warfare in primitive times. For the formation of larger and more complex social aggregates, only two methods are practicable,--conquest or federation. Greek attempts at employing the higher method, that of federation. The Athenian hegemony and its overthrow. The Achaian and Aetolian leagues. In a low stage of political development the Roman method of conquest with incorporation was the only one practicable. Peculiarities of the Roman conquest of Italy. Causes of the universal dominion of Rome. Advantages and disadvantages of this dominion:--on the one hand the pax romana, and the breaking down of primitive local superstitions and prejudices; on the other hand the partial extinction of local self-government. Despotism inevitable in the absence of representation. Causes of the political failure of the Roman system. Partial reversion of Europe, between the fifth and eleventh centuries, towards a more primitive type of social structure. Power of Rome still wielded through the Church and the imperial jurisprudence. Preservation of local self-government in England, and at the two ends of the Rhine. The Dutch and Swiss federations. The lesson to be learned from Switzerland. Federation on a great scale could only be attempted successfully by men of English political training, when working without let or hindrance in a vast country not preoccupied by an old civilization. Without local self-government a great Federal Union is impossible. Illustrations from American history. Difficulty of the problem, and failure of the early attempts at federation in New England. Effects of the war for independence. The "Articles of Confederation" and the

"Constitution." Pacific implications of American federalism.

III.

"_MANIFEST DESTINY._"

The Americans boast of the bigness of their country. How to "bound" the United States. "Manifest Destiny" of the "Anglo-Saxon Race." The term "Anglo-Saxon" slovenly and misleading. Statements relating to the "English Race" have a common interest for Americans and for Englishmen. Work of the English race in the world. The prime feature of civilization is the diminution of warfare, which becomes possible only through the formation of great political aggregates in which the parts retain their local and individual freedom. In the earlier stages of civilization, the possibility of peace can be guaranteed only through war, but the preponderant military strength is gradually concentrated in the hands of the most pacific communities, and by the continuance of this process the permanent peace of the world will ultimately be secured. Illustrations from the early struggles of European civilization with outer barbarism, and with aggressive civilizations of lower type. Greece and Persia. Keltic and Teutonic enemies of Rome. The defensible frontier of European civilization carried northward and eastward to the Rhine by Caesar; to the Oder by Charles the Great; to the Vistula by the Teutonic Knights; to the Volga and the Oxus by the Russians. Danger in the Dark Ages from Huns and Mongols on the one hand, from Mussulmans on the other. Immense increase of the area and physical strength of European civilization, which can never again be in danger from outer barbarism. Effect of all this secular turmoil upon the political institutions of Europe. It hindered the formation of closely coherent nations, and was at the same time an obstacle to the preservation of popular liberties. Tendency towards the Asiaticization of European life. Opposing influences of the Church, and of the Germanic tribal organizations. Military type of society on the Continent. Old Aryan self-government happily preserved in England. Strategic position of England favourable to the early elimination of warfare from her soil. Hence the exceptionally normal and plastic political development of the English race.

Significant coincidence of the discovery of America with the beginnings of the Protestant revolt against the asiaticizing tendency. Significance of the struggle between Spain, France, and England for the possession of an enormous area of virgin soil which should insure to the conqueror an unprecedented opportunity for future development. The race which gained control of North America must become the dominant race of the world, and its political ideas must prevail in the struggle for life. Moral significance of the rapid increase of the English race in America. Fallacy of the notion that centralized governments are needed for very large nations. It is only through federalism, combined with local self-government, that the stability of so huge an aggregate as the United States can be permanently maintained. What the American government really fought for in the late Civil War. Magnitude of the results achieved. Unprecedented military strength shown by this most pacific and industrial of peoples. Improbability of any future attempt to break up the Federal Union. Stupendous future of the English race,--in Africa, in Australia, and in the islands of the Pacific Ocean. Future of the English language. Probable further adoption of federalism. Probable effects upon Europe of industrial competition with the United States: impossibility of keeping up the present military armaments. The States of Europe will be forced, by pressure of circumstances, into some kind of federal union. A similar process will go on until the whole of mankind shall constitute a single political body, and warfare shall disappear forever from the face of the earth.

AMERICAN POLITICAL IDEAS.

I.

THE TOWN-MEETING

The traveller from the Old World, who has a few weeks at his disposal for a visit to the United States, usually passes straight from one to another of our principal cities, such as Boston, New York, Washington, or Chicago, stopping for a day or two perhaps at Niagara Falls,--or, perhaps, after traversing a distance like that which separates England from Mesopotamia, reaches the vast table-lands of the Far West and inspects their interesting fauna of antelopes and buffaloes, red Indians and Mormons. In a journey of this sort one gets a very superficial view of the peculiarities, physical and social, which characterize the different portions of our country; and in this there is nothing to complain of, since the knowledge gained in a vacation-journey cannot well be expected to be thorough or profound. The traveller, however, who should visit the United States in a more leisurely way, with the purpose of increasing his knowledge of history and politics, would find it well to proceed somewhat differently. He would find himself richly repaid for a sojourn in some insignificant place the very name of which is unknown beyond sea,--just as Mr. Mackenzie Wallace--whose book on Russia is a model of what such books should be--got so much invaluable experience from his months of voluntary exile at Ivofka in the province of Novgorod. Out of the innumerable places which one might visit in America, there are none which would better reward such careful observation, or which are more full of interest for the comparative historian, than the rural towns and mountain villages of New England; that part of English America which is oldest in civilization (though not in actual date of settlement), and which, while most completely English in blood and in traditions, is at the same time most completely American in so far as it has most distinctly illustrated and most successfully represented those political ideas which have given to American history its chief significance in the general work of civilization.

The United States are not unfrequently spoken of as a "new country," in terms which would be appropriate if applied to Australia or New Zealand, and which are not inappropriate as applied to the vast region west of the Mississippi River, where the white man had hardly set foot before the beginning of the present century. New England, however, has a history which carries us back to the times of James I.; and while its cities are full of such bustling modern life as one sees in Liverpool or Manchester or Glasgow, its rural towns show us much that is old-fashioned in aspect,--much that one can approach in an antiquarian spirit. We are there introduced to a phase of social life which is highly interesting on its own account and which has played an important part in the world, yet which, if not actually passing away, is at least becoming so rapidly modified as to afford a theme for grave reflections to those who have learned how to appreciate its value. As any far-reaching change in the condition of landed property in England, due to agricultural causes, might seriously affect the position of one of the noblest and most useful aristocracies that has ever existed; so, on the other hand, as we consider the possible action of similar causes upon the personnel and upon the occupations of rural New England, we are unwillingly forced to contemplate the possibility of a deterioration in the character of the most perfect democracy the world has ever seen.

In the outward aspect of a village in Massachusetts or Connecticut, the feature which would be most likely first to impress itself upon the mind of a visitor from England is the manner in which the village is laid out and built. Neither in England nor anywhere else in western Europe have I ever met with a village of the New England type. In English villages one finds small houses closely crowded together, sometimes in blocks of ten or a dozen, and inhabited by people belonging to the lower orders of society; while the fine houses of gentlemen stand quite apart in the country, perhaps out of sight of one another, and surrounded by very extensive grounds. The origin of the village, in a mere aggregation of tenants of the lord of the manor, is thus vividly suggested. In France one is still more impressed, I think, with this closely packed structure of the village. In the New England village, on the other hand, the finer and the poorer houses stand side by side along the road. There are wide straight streets overarched with spreading elms and maples, and on either side stand the houses, with little green lawns in front, called in rustic parlance "door-yards." The finer houses may stand a thousand feet apart from their neighbours on either side, while between the poorer ones there may be intervals of from twenty to one hundred feet, but they are never found crowded together in blocks. Built in this capacious fashion, a village of a thousand inhabitants may have a main street more than a mile in length, with half a dozen crossing streets losing themselves gradually in long stretches of country road. The finest houses are not ducal palaces, but may be compared with the ordinary country-houses of gentlemen in England. The poorest houses are never hovels, such as one sees in the Scotch Highlands.

The picturesque and cosy cottage at Shottery, where Shakespeare used to do his courting, will serve very well as a sample of the humblest sort of old-fashioned New England farm-house. But most of the dwellings in the village come between these extremes. They are plain neat wooden houses, in capaciousness more like villas than cottages. A New England village street, laid out in this way, is usually very picturesque and beautiful, and it is highly characteristic. In comparing it with things in Europe, where one rarely finds anything at all like it, one must go to something very different from a village. As you stand in the Court of Heroes at Versailles and look down the broad and noble avenue that leads to Paris, the effect of the vista is much like that of a New England village street. As American villages grow into cities, the increase in the value of land usually tends to crowd the houses together into blocks as in a European city. But in some of our western cities founded and settled by people from New England, this spacious fashion of building has been retained for streets occupied by dwelling-houses. In Cleveland--a city on the southern shore of Lake Erie, with a population about equal to that of Edinburgh--there is a street some five or six miles in length and five hundred feet in width, bordered on each side with a double row of arching trees, and with handsome stone houses, of sufficient variety and freedom in architectural design, standing at intervals of from one to two hundred feet along the entire length of the street. The effect, it is needless to add, is very noble indeed. The vistas remind one of the nave and aisles of a huge cathedral.

Now this generous way in which a New England village is built is very closely associated with the historical origin of the village and with the peculiar kind of political and social life by which it is characterized. First of all, it implies abundance of land. As a rule the head of each family owns the house in which he lives and the ground on which it is built. The relation of landlord and tenant, though not unknown, is not commonly met with. No sort of social distinction or political privilege is associated with the ownership of land; and the legal differences between real and personal property, especially as regards ease of transfer, have been reduced to the smallest minimum that practical convenience will allow. Each householder, therefore, though an absolute proprietor, cannot be called a miniature lord of the manor, because there exists no permanent dependent class such as is implied in the use of such a phrase. Each larger proprietor attends in person to the cultivation of his own land, assisted perhaps by his own sons or by neighbours working for hire in the leisure left over from the care of their own smaller estates. So in the interior of the house there is usually no domestic service that is not performed by the mother of the family and the daughters. Yet in spite of this universality of manual labour, the people are as far as possible from presenting the appearance of peasants. Poor or shabbily-dressed people are rarely seen, and there is no one in the village whom it would be proper to address in a patronizing tone, or who would not consider it a gross insult to be offered a shilling. As with poverty, so with dram-drinking and with crime; all alike are conspicuous by their absence. In a village of one thousand inhabitants there will be a poor-house where five or six decrepit old people are supported at the common charge; and there will be one tavern where it is not easy to find anything stronger to drink than light beer or cider. The danger from thieves is so slight that it is not always thought necessary to fasten the outer doors of the house at night. The universality of literary culture is as remarkable as the freedom with which all persons engage in manual labour. The village of a thousand inhabitants will be very likely to have a public circulating library, in which you may find Professor Huxley's "Lay Sermons" or Sir Henry Maine's "Ancient Law": it will surely have a high-school and half a dozen schools for small children. A person unable to read and write is as great a rarity as an albino or a person with six fingers. The farmer who threshes his own corn and cuts his own firewood has very likely a piano in his family sitting-room, with the Atlantic Monthly on the table and Milton and Tennyson, Gibbon and Macaulay on his shelves, while his daughter, who has baked bread in the morning, is perhaps ready to paint on china in the afternoon. In former times theological questions largely occupied the attention of the people; and there is probably no part of the world where the Bible has been more attentively read, or where the mysteries of Christian doctrine have to so great an extent been made the subject of earnest discussion in every household. Hence we find in the New England of to-day a deep religious sense combined with singular flexibility of mind and freedom of thought.

A state of society so completely democratic as that here described has not often been found in connection with a very high and complex civilization. In contemplating these old mountain villages of New England, one descries slow modifications in the structure of society which threaten somewhat to lessen its dignity. The immense productiveness of the soil in our western states, combined with cheapness of transportation, tends to affect seriously the agricultural interests of New England as well as those of our mother-country. There is a visible tendency for farms to pass into the hands of proprietors of an inferior type to that of the former owners,--men who are content with a lower standard of comfort and culture; while the sons of the old farmers go off to the universities to prepare for a professional career, and the daughters marry merchants or lawyers in the cities. The mountain-streams of New England, too, afford so much water-power as to bring in ugly factories to disfigure the beautiful ravines, and to introduce into the community a class of people very different from the landholding descendants of the Puritans. When once a factory is established near a village, one no longer feels free to sleep with doors unbolted.

It will be long, however, I trust, before the simple, earnest and independent type of character that has been nurtured on the Blue Hills of Massachusetts and the White Hills of New Hampshire shall cease to operate like a powerful leaven upon the whole of American society. Much has been said and sung in praise of the spirit of chivalry, which, after all, as a great historian reminds us, "implies the arbitrary choice of one or two virtues, to be practised in such an exaggerated degree as to become vices, while the ordinary laws of right and wrong are forgotten." [1] Quite enough has been said, too, in discredit of Puritanism,--its narrowness of aim, its ascetic proclivities, its quaint affectations of Hebraism. Yet these things were but the symptoms of the intensity of its reverence for that grand spirit of Hebraism, of which Mr. Matthew Arnold speaks, to which we owe the Bible and Christianity. No loftier ideal has ever been conceived than that of the Puritan who would fain have made of the world a City of God. If we could sum up all that England owes to Puritanism, the story would be a great one indeed. As regards the United States, we may safely say that what is noblest in our history to-day, and of happiest augury for our social and political future, is the impress left upon the character of our people by the heroic men who came to New England early in the seventeenth century.

The settlement of New England by the Puritans occupies a peculiar position in the annals of colonization, and without understanding this we cannot properly appreciate the character of the purely democratic society which I have sought to describe. As a general rule colonies have been founded, either by governments or by private enterprise, for political or commercial reasons. The aim has been--on the part of governments--to annoy some rival power, or to get rid of criminals, or to open some new avenue of trade, or--on the part of the people--to escape from straitened circumstances at home, or to find a refuge from religious persecution. In the settlement of New England none of these motives were operative except the last, and that only to a slight extent. The Puritans who fled from Nottinghamshire to Holland in 1608, and twelve years afterwards crossed the ocean in the Mayflower, may be said to have been driven from England by persecution. But this was not the case with the Puritans who between 1630 and 1650 went from Lincolnshire, Norfolk and Suffolk, and from Dorset and Devonshire, and founded the colonies of Massachusetts and Connecticut. These men left their homes at a time when Puritanism was waxing powerful and could not be assailed with impunity. They belonged to the upper and middle classes of the society of that day, outside of the peerage. Mr. Freeman has pointed out the importance of the change by which, after the Norman Conquest, the Old-English nobility or thegnhood was pushed down into "a secondary place in the political and social scale." Of the far-reaching effects of this change upon the whole subsequent history of the English race I shall hereafter have occasion to speak. The proximate effect was that "the ancient lords of the soil, thus thrust down into the second rank, formed that great body of freeholders, the stout gentry and yeomanry of England, who were for so many ages the strength of the land." [2] It was from this ancient thegnhood that the Puritan settlers of New England were mainly descended. It is no unusual thing for a

Massachusetts family to trace its pedigree to a lord of the manor in the thirteenth or fourteenth century. The leaders of the New England emigration were country gentlemen of good fortune, similar in position to such men as Hampden and Cromwell; a large proportion of them had taken degrees at Cambridge. The rank and file were mostly intelligent and prosperous yeomen. The lowest ranks of society were not represented in the emigration; and all idle, shiftless, or disorderly people were rigorously refused admission into the new communities, the early history of which was therefore singularly free from anything like riot or mutiny. To an extent unparalleled, therefore, in the annals of colonization, the settlers of New England were a body of picked men. Their Puritanism was the natural outcome of their free-thinking, combined with an earnestness of character which could constrain them to any sacrifices needful for realizing their high ideal of life. They gave up pleasant homes in England, and they left them with no feeling of rancour towards their native land, in order that, by dint of whatever hardship, they might establish in the American wilderness what should approve itself to their judgment as a god-fearing community. It matters little that their conceptions were in some respects narrow. In the unflinching adherence to duty which prompted their enterprise, and in the sober intelligence with which it was carried out, we have, as I said before, the key to what is best in the history of the American people.

Out of such a colonization as that here described nothing but a democratic society could very well come, save perhaps in case of a scarcity of arable land. Between the country gentleman and the yeoman who has become a landed proprietor, the difference is not great enough to allow the establishment of permanent distinctions, social or political. Immediately on their arrival in New England, the settlers proceeded to form for themselves a government as purely democratic as any that has ever been seen in the world. Instead of scattering about over the country, the requirements of education and of public worship, as well as of defence against Indian attacks, obliged them to form small village communities. As these villages multiplied, the surface of the country came to be laid out in small districts (usually from six to ten miles in length and breadth) called townships. Each township contained its village together with the woodlands surrounding it. In later days two or more villages have often grown up within the limits of the same township, and the road from one village to another is sometimes bordered with homesteads and cultivated fields throughout nearly its whole length. In the neighbourhood of Boston villages and small towns crowd closely together for twenty miles in every direction; and all these will no doubt by and by grow together into a vast and complicated city, in somewhat the same way that London has grown.

From the outset the government of the township was vested in the TOWN-MEETING,--an institution which in its present form is said to be peculiar to New England, but which, as we shall see, has close analogies with local self-governing bodies in other ages and countries. Once in each year--usually in the month of March--a meeting is held, at which every adult male residing within the limits of the township is expected to be present, and is at liberty to address the meeting or to vote upon any question that may come up.

In the first years of the colonies it seems to have been attempted to hold town-meetings every month, and to discuss all the affairs of the community in these assemblies; but this was soon found to be a cumbrous way of transacting public business, and as early as 1635 we find selectmen chosen to administer the affairs of the township during the intervals between the assemblies. As the system has perfected itself, at each annual town-meeting there are chosen not less than three or more than nine selectmen, according to the size of the township. Besides these, there are chosen a town-clerk, a town-treasurer, a school-committee, assessors of taxes, overseers of the poor, constables, surveyors of highways, fence-viewers, and other officers. In very small townships the selectmen themselves may act as assessors of taxes or overseers of the poor. The selectmen may appoint police-officers if such are required; they may act as a Board of Health; in addition to sundry specific duties too numerous to mention here, they have the general superintendence of all public business save such as is expressly assigned to the other officers; and whenever circumstances may seem to require it they are authorized to call a town-meeting. The selectmen are thus the principal town-magistrates; and through the annual election their responsibility to the town is maintained at the maximum. Yet in many New England towns re-election of the same persons year after year has very commonly prevailed. I know of an instance where the office of town-clerk was filled by three members of one family during one hundred and fourteen consecutive years.

Besides choosing executive officers, the town-meeting has the power of enacting by-laws, of making appropriations of money for town-purposes, and of providing for miscellaneous emergencies by what might be termed special legislation. Besides the annual meeting held in the spring for transacting all this local business, the selectmen are required to call a meeting in the autumn of each year for the election of state and county officers, each second year for the election of representatives to the federal Congress, and each fourth year for the election of the President of the United States.

It only remains to add that, as an assembly of the whole people becomes impracticable in a large community, so when the population of a township has grown to ten or twelve thousand, the town-meeting is discontinued, the town is incorporated as a city, and its affairs are managed by a mayor, a board of aldermen, and a common council, according to the system adopted in London in the reign of Edward I. In America, therefore, the distinction between cities and towns has nothing to do with the presence or absence of a cathedral, but refers solely to differences in the communal or municipal government. In the city the common council, as a representative body, replaces (in a certain sense) the town-meeting; a representative government is substituted for a pure democracy. But the city officers, like the selectmen of towns, are elected annually; and in no case (I believe) has municipal government fallen into the hands of a self-perpetuating body, as it has done in so many instances in England owing to the unwise policy pursued by the Tudors and Stuarts in their grants of charters.

It is only in New England that the township system is to be found in its completeness. In several southern and western states the administrative unit is the county, and local affairs are managed by county commissioners elected by the people. Elsewhere we find a mixture of the county and township systems. In some of the western states settled by New England people, town-meetings are held, though their powers are somewhat less extensive than in New England. In the settlement of Virginia it was attempted to copy directly the parishes and vestries, boroughs and guilds of England. But in the southern states generally the great size of the plantations and the wide dispersion of the population hindered the growth of towns, so that it was impossible to have an administrative unit smaller than the county. As Tocqueville said fifty years ago, "the farther south we go the less active does the business of the township or parish become; the population exercises a less immediate influence on affairs; the power of the elected magistrate is augmented and that of the election diminished, while the public spirit of the local communities is less quickly awakened and less influential." This is almost equally true to-day; yet with all these differences in local organization, there is no part of our country in which the spirit of local self-government can be called weak or uncertain. I have described the Town-meeting as it exists in the states where it first grew up and has since chiefly flourished. But something very like the "town-meeting principle" lies at the bottom of all the political life of the United States. To maintain vitality in the centre without sacrificing it in the parts; to preserve tranquillity in the mutual relations of forty powerful states, while keeping the people everywhere as far as possible in direct contact with the government; such is the political problem which the American Union exists for the purpose of solving; and of this great truth every American citizen is supposed to have some glimmering, however crude.

It has been said that the town-governments of New England were established without any conscious reference to precedent; but, however this may be, they are certainly not without precedents and analogies, to enumerate which will carry us very far back in the history of the Aryan world. At the beginning of his essay on the "Growth of the English Constitution," Mr. Freeman gives an eloquent account of the May assemblies of Uri and Appenzell, when the whole people elect their magistrates for the year and vote upon amendments to the old laws or upon the adoption of new ones. Such a sight Mr. Freeman seems to think can be seen nowhere but in

Switzerland, and he reckons it among the highest privileges of his life to have looked upon it. But I am unable to see in what respect the town-meeting in Massachusetts differs from the Landesgemeinde or cantonal assembly in Switzerland, save that it is held in a town-hall and not in the open air, that it is conducted with somewhat less of pageantry, and that the freemen who attend do not carry arms even by way of ceremony. In the Swiss assembly, as Mr. Freeman truly observes, we see exemplified the most democratic phase of the old Teutonic constitution as described in the "Germania" of Tacitus, "the earliest picture which history can give us of the political and social being of our own forefathers." The same remark, in precisely the same terms, would be true of the town-meetings of New England. Political institutions, on the White Mountains and on the Alps, not only closely resemble each other, but are connected by strict bonds of descent from a common original.

The most primitive self-governing body of which we have any knowledge is the village-community of the ancient Teutons, of which such strict counterparts are found in other parts of the Aryan world as to make it apparent that in its essential features it must be an inheritance from prehistoric Aryan antiquity. In its Teutonic form the primitive village-community (or rather, the spot inhabited by it) is known as the Mark,--that is, a place defined by a boundary-line. One characteristic of the mark-community is that all its free members are in theory supposed to be related to each other through descent from a common progenitor; and in this respect the mark-community agrees with the gens, [Greek: _ginos_], or clan. The earliest form of political union in the world is one which rests, not upon territorial contiguity, but upon I blood-relationship, either real or assumed through the legal fiction of adoption. In the lowest savagery blood-relationship is the only admissible or conceivable ground for sustained common action among groups of men. Among peoples which wander about, supporting themselves either by hunting, or at a somewhat more advanced stage of development by the rearing of flocks and herds, a group of men, thus permanently associated through ties of blood-relationship, is what we call a clan. When by the development of agricultural pursuits the nomadic mode of life is brought to an end, when the clan remains stationary upon some piece of territory surrounded by a strip of forest-land, or other boundaries natural or artificial, then the clan becomes a mark-community. The profound linguistic researches of Pictet, Fick, and others have made it probable that at the time when the Old-Aryan language was broken up into the dialects from which the existing languages of Europe are descended, the Aryan tribes were passing from a purely pastoral stage of barbarism into an incipient agricultural stage, somewhat like that which characterized the Iroquois tribes in America in the seventeenth century. The comparative study of institutions leads to results in harmony with this view, showing us the mark-community of our Teutonic ancestors with the clear traces of its origin in the more primitive clan; though, with Mr. Kemble, I do not doubt that by the time of Tacitus the German tribes had long since reached the agricultural stage.

Territorially the old Teutonic mark consisted of three divisions. There was the village mark, where the people lived in houses crowded closely together, no doubt for defensive purposes; there was the arable mark, divided into as many lots as there were householders; and there was the common mark, or border-strip of untilled land, wherein all the inhabitants of the village had common rights of pasturage and of cutting firewood. All this land originally was the property not of any one family or individual, but of the community. The study of the mark carries us back to a time when there may have been private property in weapons, utensils, or trinkets, but not in real estate.[3] Of the three kinds of land the common mark, save where curtailed or usurped by lords in the days of feudalism, has generally remained public property to this day. The pleasant green commons or squares which occur in the midst of towns and cities in England and the United States most probably originated from the coalescence of adjacent mark-communities, whereby the border-land used in common by all was brought into the centre of the new aggregate. In towns of modern date this origin of the common is of course forgotten, and in accordance with the general law by which the useful thing after discharging its functions survives for purposes of ornament, it is introduced as a pleasure-ground. In old towns of New England, however, the little park where boys play ball or children and nurses "take the air" was once the common pasture of the town. Even Boston Common did not entirely cease to be a grazing-field until 1830. It was in the village-mark, or assemblage of homesteads, that private property in real estate naturally began. In the Russian villages to-day the homesteads are private property, while the cultivated land is owned in common. This was the case with the arable mark of our ancestors. The arable mark belonged to the community, and was temporarily divided into as many fields as there were households, though the division was probably not into equal parts: more likely, as in Russia to-day, the number of labourers in each household was taken into the account; and at irregular intervals, as fluctuations in population seemed to require it, a thorough-going redivision was effected. In carrying out such divisions and redivisions, as well as in all matters relating to village, ploughed field, or pasture, the mark-community was a law unto itself. Though individual freedom was by no means considerable, the legal existence of the individual being almost entirely merged in that of his clan, the mark-community was a completely self-governing body. The assembly of the mark-men, or members of the community, allotted land for tillage, determined the law or declared the custom as to methods of tillage, fixed the dates for sowing and reaping, voted upon the admission of new families into the village, and in general transacted what was then regarded as the public business of the community. In all essential respects this village assembly or _mark-mote_ would seem to have resembled the town-meetings of New England.

Such was the mark-community of the ancient Teutons, as we gather partly from hints afforded by Tacitus and partly from the comparative study of English, German, and Scandinavian institutions. In Russia and in Hindustan we find the same primitive form of social organization existing with very little change at the present day. Alike in Hindu and in Russian village-communities we find the group of habitations, each despotically ruled by a _pater-familias;_ we find the pasture-land owned and enjoyed in common; and we find the arable land divided into separate lots, which are cultivated according to minute regulations established by the community. But in India the occasional redistribution of lots survives only in a few localities, and as a mere tradition in others; the arable mark has become private property, as well as the homesteads. In Russia, on the other hand, re-allotments occur at irregular intervals averaging something like fifteen years. In India the local government is carried on in some places by a Council of Village Elders, and in other places by a Headman whose office is sometimes described as hereditary, but is more probably elective, the choice being confined, as in the case of the old Teutonic kingship, to the members of a particular family. In the Russian village, on the other hand, the government is conducted by an assembly at which every head of a household is expected to be present and vote on all matters of public concern. This assembly elects the Village Elder, or chief executive officer, the tax-collector, the watchman, and the communal herd-boy; it directs the allotment of the arable land; and in general matters of local legislation its power is as great as that of the New England town-meeting,--in some respects perhaps even greater, since the precise extent of its powers has never been determined by legislation, and (according to Mr. Wallace) "there is no means of appealing against its decisions." To those who are in the habit of regarding Russia simply as a despotically-governed country, such a statement may seem surprising. To those who, because the Russian government is called a bureaucracy, have been led to think of it as analogous to the government of France under the Old Regime, it may seem incredible that the decisions of a village-assembly should not admit of appeal to a higher authority. But in point of fact, no two despotic governments could be less alike than that of modern Russia and that of France under the Old Regime. The Russian government is autocratic inasmuch as over the larger part of the country it has simply succeeded to the position of the Mongolian khans who from the thirteenth to the fifteenth century held the Russian people in subjection. This Mongolian government was--to use a happy distinction suggested by Sir Henry Maine--a tax-taking despotism, not a legislative despotism. The conquerors exacted tribute, but did not interfere with the laws and customs of the subject people. When the Russians drove out the Mongols they exchanged a despotism which they hated for one in which they felt a national pride, but in one curious respect the position of the people with reference to their rulers has remained the same. The imperial government exacts from each village-community a tax in gross, for which the community as a whole is responsible, and which may or may not be oppressive in amount; but the government has never interfered with local legislation or with local customs. Thus in the mir, or village-community, the Russians still retain an element of sound political life, the importance of which appears when we consider that five-sixths of the population of European Russia is comprised in these communities. The tax assessed upon them by the imperial government is, however, a feature which--even more than their imperfect system of property and their low grade of mental culture--separates them by a world-wide interval from the New England township, to the primeval embryonic stage of which they correspond.

From these illustrations we see that the mark, or self-governing village-community, is an institution which must be referred back to early Aryan times. Whether the mark ever existed in England, in anything like the primitive form in which it is seen in the Russian mir, is doubtful. Professor Stubbs (one of the greatest living authorities on such a subject) is inclined to think that the Teutonic settlers of Britain had passed beyond this stage before they migrated from Germany.[4] Nevertheless the traces of the mark, as all admit, are plentiful enough in England; and some of its features have survived down to modern times. In the great number of town-names that are formed from patronymics, such as Walsingham "the home of the Walsings," Harlington "the town of the Harlings," etc.,[5] we have unimpeachable evidence of a time when the town was regarded as the dwelling-place of a clan. Indeed, the comparative rarity of the word mark in English laws, charters, and local names (to which Professor Stubbs alludes) may be due to the fact that the word town has precisely the same meaning. Mark means originally the belt of waste land encircling the village, and secondarily the village with its periphery. Town means originally a hedge or enclosure, and secondarily the spot that is enclosed: the modern German zaun, a "hedge," preserves the original meaning. But traces of the mark in England are not found in etymology alone. I have already alluded to the origin of the "common" in English towns. What is still more important is that in some parts of England cultivation in common has continued until quite recently. The local legislation of the mark appears in the tunscipesmot,--a word which is simply Old-English for "town-meeting." In the shires where the Danes acquired a firm foothold, the township was often called a "by"; and it had the power of enacting its own "by-laws" or town-laws, as New England townships have to-day. But above all, the assembly of the markmen has left vestiges of itself in the constitution of the parish and the manor. The mark or township, transformed by the process of feudalization, becomes the manor. The process of feudalization, throughout western Europe in general, was no doubt begun by the institution of Benefices, or "grants of Roman provincial land by the chieftains of the" Teutonic "tribes which overran the Roman Empire; such grants being conferred on their associates upon certain conditions, of which the commonest was military service." [6] The feudal regime naturally reached its most complete development in France, which affords the most perfect example of a Roman territory overrun and permanently held in possession by Teutonic conquerors. Other causes assisted the process, the most potent perhaps being the chaotic condition of European society during the break-up of the Carolingian Empire and the Scandinavian and Hungarian invasions. Land was better protected when held of a powerful chieftain than when held in one's own right; and hence the practice of commendation, by which free allodial proprietors were transformed into the tenants of a lord, became fashionable and was gradually extended to all kinds of estates. In England the effects of feudalization were different from what they were in France, but the process was still carried very far, especially under the Norman kings. The theory grew up that all the public land in the kingdom was the king's waste, and that all landholders were the king's tenants. Similarly in every township the common land was the lord's waste and the landholders were the lord's tenants. Thus the township became transformed into the manor. Yet even by such a change as this the townsmen or tenants of the manor did not in England lose their self-government. "The encroachments of the lord," as Sir Henry Maine observes, "were in proportion to the want of certainty in the rights of the community." The lord's proprietorship gave him no authority to disturb customary rights. The old township-assembly partially survived in the Court Baron, Court Leet, and Customary Court of the Manor; and in these courts the arrangements for the common husbandry were determined.

This metamorphosis of the township into the manor, however, was but partial: along with it went the partial metamorphosis of the township into the parish, or district assigned to a priest. Professor Stubbs has pointed out that "the boundaries of the parish and the township or townships with which it coincides are generally the same: in small parishes the idea and even the name of township is frequently, at the present day, sunk in that of the parish; and all the business that is not manorial is despatched in vestry-meetings, which are however primarily meetings of the township for church purposes." [7] The parish officers, including overseers of the poor, assessors, and way-wardens, are still elected in vestry-meeting by the freemen of the township. And while the jurisdiction of the manorial courts has been defined by charter, or by the customary law existing at the time of the manorial grant, "all matters arising outside that jurisdiction come under the management of the vestry."

In England, therefore, the free village-community, though perhaps nowhere found in its primitive integrity, has nevertheless survived in partially transfigured forms which have played no unimportant part in the history of the English people. In one shape or another the assembly of freemen for purposes of local legislation has always existed. The Puritans who colonized New England, therefore, did not invent the town-meeting. They were familiar already with the proceedings of the vestry-meeting and the manorial courts, but they were severed now from church and from aristocracy. So they had but to discard the ecclesiastical and lordly terminology, with such limitations as they involved, and to reintegrate the separate jurisdictions into one,--and forthwith the old assembly of the township, founded in immemorial tradition, but revivified by new thoughts and purposes gained through ages of political training, emerged into fresh life and entered upon a more glorious career.

It is not to an audience which speaks the English language that I need to argue the point that the preservation of local self-government is of the highest importance for the maintenance of a rich and powerful national life. As we contemplate the vicissitudes of local self-government in the various portions of the Aryan world, we see the contrasted fortunes of France and England illustrating for us most forcibly the significance of this truth. For the preservation of local self-government in England various causes may be assigned; but of these there are two which may be cited as especially prominent. In the first place, owing to the peculiar circumstances of the Teutonic settlement of Britain, the civilization of England previous to the Norman Conquest was but little affected by Roman ideas or institutions. In the second place the thrusting down of the old thegnhood by the Norman Conquest (to which I have already alluded) checked the growth of a noblesse or adel of the continental type,--a nobility raised above the common people like a separate caste. For the old thegnhood, which might have grown into such a caste, was pushed down into a secondary position, and the peerage which arose after the Conquest was something different from a noblesse. It was primarily a nobility of office rather than of rank or privilege. The peers were those men who retained the right of summons to the Great Council, or Witenagemote, which has survived as the House of Lords. The peer was therefore the holder of a legislative and judicial office, which only one of his children could inherit, from the very nature of the case, and which none of his children could share with him. Hence the brothers and younger children of a peer were always commoners, and their interests were not remotely separated from those of other commoners. Hence after the establishment of a House of Commons, their best chance for a political career lay in representing the interests of the people in the lower house. Hence between the upper and lower strata of English society there has always been kept up a circulation or interchange of ideas and interests, and the effect of this upon English history has been prodigious. While on the continent a sovereign like Charles the Bold could use his nobility to extinguish the liberties of the merchant towns of Flanders, nothing of the sort was ever possible in England. Throughout the Middle Ages, in every contest between the people and the crown, the weight of the peerage was thrown into the scale in favour of popular liberties. But for this peculiar position of the peerage we might have had no Earl Simon; it is largely through it that representative government and local liberties have been preserved to the English race.

In France the course of events has brought about very different results. I shall defer to my next lecture the consideration of the vicissitudes of local self-government under the Roman Empire, because that point is really incident upon the study of the formation of vast national aggregates. Suffice it now to say that when the Teutons overcame Gaul, they became rulers over a population which had been subjected for five centuries to that slow but mighty process of trituration which the Empire everywhere brought to bear upon local self-government. While the Teutons in Britain, moreover, enslaved their slightly romanized subjects and gave little heed to their language, religion, or customs; the Teutons in Gaul, on the other hand, quickly adopted the language and religion of their intensely romanized subjects and acquired to some extent their way of looking at things. Hence in the early history of France there was no such stubborn mass of old Aryan liberties to be dealt with as in the early history of England. Nor was there any powerful middle class distributed through the country to defend such liberties as existed. Beneath the turbulent throng of Teutonic nobles, among whom the king was only the most exalted and not always the strongest, there lay the Gallo-Roman population which had so long been accustomed to be ruled without representation by a distant government exercising its authority through innumerable prefects. Such Teutonic rank and file as there was became absorbed into this population; and except in sundry chartered towns there was nothing like a social stratum interposed between the nobles and the common people.

The slow conversion of the feudal monarchy of the early Capetians into the absolute despotism of Louis XIV. was accomplished by the king gradually conquering his vassals one after another, and adding their domains to his own. As one vassal territory after another was added to the royal domain, the king sent prefects, responsible only to himself, to administer its local affairs, sedulously crushing out, so far as possible, the last vestiges of self-government. The nobles, deprived of their provincial rule, in great part flocked to Paris to become idle courtiers. The means for carrying on the gigantic machinery of centralized administration, and for supporting the court in its follies, were wrung from the groaning peasantry with a cynical indifference like that with which tribute is extorted by barbaric chieftains from a conquered enemy. And thus came about that abominable state of things which a century since was abruptly ended by one of the fiercest convulsions of modern times. The prodigious superiority--in respect to national vitality--of a freely governed country over one that is governed by a centralized despotism, is nowhere more brilliantly illustrated than in the contrasted fortunes of France and England as colonizing nations. When we consider the declared rivalry between France and England in their plans for colonizing the barbarous regions of the earth, when we consider that the military power of the two countries has been not far from equal, and that France has at times shown herself a maritime power by no means to be despised, it seems to me that her overwhelming and irretrievable defeat by England in the struggle for colonial empire is one of the most striking and one of the most instructive facts in all modern history. In my lectures of last year (at University College) I showed that, in the struggle for the possession of North America, where the victory of England was so decisive as to settle the question for all coming time, the causes of the French failure are very plainly to be seen. The French colony in Canada was one of the most complete examples of a despotic government that the world has ever seen. All the autocratic and bureaucratic ideas of Louis XIV. were here carried out without let or hindrance. It would be incredible, were it not attested by such abundant evidence, that the affairs of any people could be subjected to such minute and sleepless supervision as were the affairs of the French colonists in Canada. A man could not even build his own house, or rear his own cattle, or sow his own seed, or reap his own grain, save under the supervision of prefects acting under instructions from the home government. No one was allowed to enter or leave the colony without permission, not from the colonists but from the king. No farmer could visit Montreal or Quebec without permission. No Huguenot could set his foot on Canadian soil. No public meetings of any kind were tolerated, nor were there any means of giving expression to one's opinions on any subject. The details of all this, which may be read in Mr. Parkman's admirable work on "The Old Regime in Canada," make a wonderful chapter of history. Never was a colony, moreover, so loaded with bounties, so fostered, petted, and protected. The result was absolute paralysis, political and social. When after a century of irritation and skirmishing the French in Canada came to a life-and-death struggle with the self-governing colonists of New England, New York, and Virginia, the result for the French power in America was instant and irretrievable annihilation. The town-meeting pitted against the bureaucracy was like a Titan overthrowing a cripple. The historic lesson owes its value to the fact that this ruin of the French scheme of colonial empire was due to no accidental circumstances, but was involved in the very nature of the French political system. Obviously it is impossible for a people to plant beyond sea a colony which shall be self-supporting, unless it has retained intact the power of self-government at home. It is to the self-government of England, and to no lesser cause, that we are to look for the secret of that boundless vitality which has given to men of English speech the uttermost parts of the earth for an inheritance. The conquest of Canada first demonstrated this truth, and when--in the two following lectures--we shall have made some approach towards comprehending its full import, we shall all, I think, be ready to admit that the triumph of Wolfe marks the greatest turning-point as yet discernible in modern history.

II.

THE FEDERAL UNION.

The great history of Thukydides, which after twenty-three centuries still ranks (in spite of Mr. Cobden) among our chief text-books of political wisdom, has often seemed to me one of the most mournful books in the world. At no other spot on the earth's surface, and at no other time in the career of mankind, has the human intellect flowered with such luxuriance as at Athens during the eighty-five years which intervened between the victory of Marathon and the defeat of Aeospotamos. In no other like interval of time, and in no other community of like dimensions, has so much work been accomplished of which we can say with truth that it is [Greek: ktaema es aei],--an eternal possession. It is impossible to conceive of a day so distant, or an era of culture so exalted, that the lessons taught by Athens shall cease to be of value, or that the writings of her great thinkers shall cease to be read with fresh profit and delight. We understand these things far better to-day than did those monsters of erudition in the sixteenth century who studied the classics for philological purposes mainly. Indeed, the older the world grows, the more varied our experience of practical politics, the more comprehensive our survey of universal history, the stronger our grasp upon the comparative method of inquiry, the more brilliant is the light thrown upon that brief day of Athenian greatness, and the more wonderful and admirable does it all seem. To see this glorious community overthrown, shorn of half its virtue (to use the Homeric phrase), and thrust down into an inferior position in the world, is a mournful spectacle indeed. And the book which sets before us, so impartially yet so eloquently, the innumerable petty misunderstandings and contemptible jealousies which brought about this direful result, is one of the most mournful of books.

We may console ourselves, however, for the premature overthrow of the power of Athens, by the reflection that that power rested upon political conditions which could not in any case have been permanent or even long-enduring. The entire political system of ancient Greece, based as it was upon the idea of the sovereign independence of each single city, was one which could not fail sooner or later to exhaust itself through chronic anarchy. The only remedy lay either in some kind of permanent federation, combined with representative government; or else in what we might call "incorporation and assimilation," after the Roman fashion. But the incorporation of one town with another, though effected with brilliant results in the early history of Attika, involved such a disturbance of all the associations which in the Greek mind clustered about the conception of a city that it was quite impracticable on any large or general scale. Schemes of federal union were put into operation, though too late to be of avail against the assaults of Macedonia and Rome. But as for the principle of representation, that seems to have been an invention of the Teutonic mind; no statesman of antiquity, either in Greece or at Rome, seems to have conceived the idea of a city sending delegates armed with plenary powers to represent its interests in a general legislative assembly. To the Greek statesmen, no doubt, this too would have seemed derogatory to the dignity of the sovereign city.

This feeling with which the ancient Greek statesmen, and to some extent the Romans also, regarded the city, has become almost incomprehensible to the modern mind, so far removed are we from the political circumstances which made such a feeling possible. Teutonic civilization, indeed, has never passed through a stage in which the foremost position has been held by civic communities. Teutonic civilization passed directly from the stage of tribal into that of national organization, before any Teutonic city had acquired sufficient importance to have claimed autonomy for itself; and at the time when Teutonic nationalities were forming, moreover, all the cities in Europe had so long been accustomed to recognize a master outside of them in the person of the Roman emperor that the very tradition of civic autonomy, as it existed in ancient Greece, had become extinct. This difference between the political basis of Teutonic and of Greco-Roman civilization is one of which it would be difficult to exaggerate the importance; and when thoroughly understood it goes farther, perhaps, than anything else towards accounting for the successive failures of the Greek and Roman political systems, and towards inspiring us with confidence in the future stability of the political system which has been wrought out by the genius of the English race.

We saw, in the preceding lecture, how the most primitive form of political association known to have existed is that of the clan, or group of families held together by ties of descent from a common ancestor. We saw how the change from a nomadic to a stationary mode of life, attendant upon the adoption of agricultural pursuits, converted the clan into a mark or village-community, something like those which exist to-day in Russia. The political progress of primitive society seems to have consisted largely in the coalescence of these small groups into larger groups. The first series of compound groups resulting from the coalescence of adjacent marks is that which was known in nearly all Teutonic lands as the hundred, in Athens as the [Greek: _phratria_] or brotherhood, in Rome as the curia. Yet alongside of the Roman group called the curia there is a group whose name, the century, exactly translates the name of the Teutonic group; and, as Mr. Freeman says, it is difficult to believe that the Roman century did not at the outset in some way correspond to the Teutonic hundred as a stage in political organization. But both these terms, as we know them in history, are survivals from some prehistoric state of things; and whether they were originally applied to a hundred of houses, or of families, or of warriors, we do not know.[8] M. Geffroy, in his interesting essay on the Germania of Tacitus, suggests that the term canton may have a similar origin.[9] The outlines of these primitive groups are, however, more obscure than those of the more primitive mark, because in most cases they have been either crossed and effaced or at any rate diminished in importance by the more highly compounded groups which came next in order of formation. Next above the hundred, in order of composition, comes the group known in ancient Italy as thepagus, in Attika perhaps as the deme, in Germany and at first in England as the gau or ga, at a later date in England as the shire. Whatever its name, this group answers to the tribe regarded as settled upon a certain determinate territory. Just as in the earlier nomadic life the aggregation of clans makes ultimately the tribe, so in the more advanced agricultural life of our Aryan ancestors the aggregation of marks or village-communities makes ultimately the gau or shire. Properly speaking, the name shire is descriptive of division and not of aggregation; but this term came into use in England after the historic order of formation had been forgotten, and when the shire was looked upon as a piece of some larger whole, such as the kingdom of Mercia or Wessex. Historically, however, the shire was not made, like the departments of modern France, by the division of the kingdom for administrative purposes, but the kingdom was made by the union of shires that were previously autonomous. In the primitive process of aggregation, the shire or gau, governed by its witenagemote or "meeting of wise men," and by its chief magistrate who was called ealdorman in time of peace and heretoga, "army-leader," dux, or duke, in time of war,--the shire, I say, in this form, is the largest and most complex political body we find previous to the formation of kingdoms and nations. But in saying this, we have already passed beyond the point at which we can include in the same general formula the process of political development in Teutonic countries on the one hand and in Greece and Rome on the other. Up as far as the formation of the tribe, territorially regarded, the parallelism is preserved; but at this point there begins an all-important divergence. In the looser and more diffused society of the rural Teutons, the tribe is spread over a shire, and the aggregation of shires makes a kingdom, embracing cities, towns, and rural districts held together by similar bonds of relationship to the central governing power. But in the society of the old Greeks and Italians, the aggregation of tribes, crowded together on fortified hill-tops, makes the Ancient City,--a very different thing, indeed, from the modern city of later-Roman or Teutonic foundation. Let us consider, for a moment, the difference.

Sir Henry Maine tells us that in Hindustan nearly all the great towns and cities have arisen either from the simple expansion or from the expansion and coalescence of primitive village-communities; and such as have not arisen in this way, including some of the greatest of Indian cities, have grown up about the intrenched camps of the Mogul emperors.[10] The case has been just the same in modern Europe. Some famous cities of England and Germany--such as Chester and Lincoln, Strasburg and Maintz,--grew up about the camps of the Roman legions. But in general the Teutonic city has been formed by the expansion and coalescence of thickly-peopled townships and hundreds. In the United States nearly all cities have come from the growth and expansion of villages, with such occasional cases of coalescence as that of Boston with Roxbury and Charlestown. Now and then a city has been laid out as a city ab initio, with full consciousness of its purpose, as a man would build a house; and this was the case not merely with Martin Chuzzlewit's "Eden," but with the city of Washington, the seat of our federal government. But, to go back to the early ages of England--the country which best exhibits the normal development of Teutonic institutions--the point which I wish especially to emphasize is this: _in no case does the city appear as equivalent to the dwelling-place of a tribe or of a confederation of tribes_. In no case does citizenship, or burghership, appear to rest upon the basis of a real or assumed community of descent from a single real or mythical progenitor. In the primitive mark, as we have seen, the bond which kept the community together and constituted it a political unit was the bond of blood-relationship, real or assumed; but this was not the case with the city or borough. The city did not correspond with the tribe, as the mark corresponded with the clan. The aggregation of clans into tribes corresponded with the aggregation of marks, not into cities but into shires. The multitude of compound political units, by the further compounding of which a nation was to be formed, did not consist of cities but of shires. The city was simply a point in the shire distinguished by greater density of population. The relations sustained by the thinly-peopled rural townships and hundreds to the general government of the shire were co-ordinate with the relations sustained to the same government by those thickly-peopled townships and hundreds which upon their coalescence were known as cities or boroughs. Of course I am speaking now in a broad and general way, and without reference to such special privileges or immunities as cities and boroughs frequently obtained by royal charter in feudal times. Such special privileges--as for instance the exemption of boroughs from the ordinary sessions of the county court, under Henry I.[11]--were in their nature grants from an external source, and were in nowise inherent in the position or mode of origin of the Teutonic city. And they were, moreover, posterior in date to that embryonic period of national growth of which I am now speaking. They do not affect in any way the correctness of my general statement, which is sufficiently illustrated by the fact that the oldest shire-motes, or county-assemblies, were attended by representatives from all the townships and hundreds in the shire, whether such townships and hundreds formed parts of boroughs or not.

Very different from this was the embryonic growth of political society in ancient Greece and Italy. There the aggregation of clans into tribes and confederations of tribes resulted directly, as we have seen, in the City. There burghership, with its political and social rights and duties, had its theoretical basis in descent from a common ancestor, or from a small group of closely-related common ancestors. The group of fellow-citizens was associated through its related groups of ancestral household-deities, and through religious rites performed in common to which it would have been sacrilege to have admitted a stranger. Thus the Ancient City was a religious as well as a political body, and in either character it was complete in itself and it was sovereign. Thus in ancient Greece and Italy the primitive clan-assembly or township-meeting did not grow by aggregation into the assembly of the shire, but it developed into the comitia or ecclesia of the city. The chief magistrate was not the ealdorman of early English history, but the rex or basileus who combined in himself the functions of king, general, and priest. Thus, too, there was a severance, politically, between city and country such as the Teutonic world has never known. The rural districts surrounding a city might be subject to it, but could neither share its franchise nor claim a co-ordinate franchise with it. Athens, indeed, at an early period, went so far as to incorporate with itself Eleusis and Marathon and the other rural towns of Attika. In this one respect Athens transgressed the bounds of ancient civic organization, and no doubt it gained greatly in power thereby. But generally in the Hellenic world the rural population in the neighbourhood of a great city were mere [Greek: _perioikoi_], or "dwellers in the vicinity"; the inhabitants of the city who had moved thither from some other city, both they and their descendants, were mere [Greek: metoikoi], or "dwellers in the place"; and neither the one class nor the other could acquire the rights and privileges of citizenship. A revolution, indeed, went on at Athens, from the time of Solon to the time of Kleisthenes, which essentially modified the old tribal divisions and admitted to the franchise all such families resident from time immemorial as did not belong to the tribes of eupatrids by whom the city was founded. But this change once accomplished, the civic exclusiveness of Athens remained very much what it was before. The popular assembly was enlarged, and public harmony was secured; but Athenian burghership still remained a privilege which could not be acquired by the native of any other city. Similar revolutions, with a similarly limited purpose and result, occurred at Sparta, Elis, and other Greek cities. At Rome, by a like revolution, the plebeians of the Capitoline and Aventine acquired parallel rights of citizenship with the patricians of the original city on the Palatine; but this revolution, as we shall presently see, had different results, leading ultimately to the overthrow of the city-system throughout the ancient world.

The deep-seated difference between the Teutonic political system based on the shire and the Greco-Roman system based on the city is now, I think, sufficiently apparent. Now from this fundamental difference have come two consequences of enormous importance,--consequences of which it is hardly too much to say that, taken together, they furnish the key to the whole history of European civilization as regarded purely from a political point of view.

The first of these consequences had no doubt a very humble origin in the mere difference between the shire and the city in territorial extent and in density of population. When people live near together it is easy for them to attend a town-meeting, and the assembly by which public business is transacted is likely to remain a primary assembly, in the true sense of the term. But when people are dispersed over a wide tract of country, the primary assembly inevitably shrinks up into an assembly of such persons as can best afford the time and trouble of attending it, or who have the strongest interest in going, or are most likely to be listened to after they get there. Distance and difficulty, and in early times danger too, keep many people away. And though a shire is not a wide tract of country for most purposes, and according to modern ideas, it was nevertheless quite wide enough in former times to bring about the result I have mentioned. In the times before the Norman conquest, if not before the completed union of England under Edgar, the shire-mote or county assembly, though in theory still a folk-mote or primary assembly, had shrunk into what was virtually a witenagemote or assembly of the most important persons in the county. But the several townships, in order to keep their fair share of control over county affairs, and not wishing to leave the matter to chance, sent to the meetings each its representatives in the persons of the town-reeve and four "discreet men." I believe it has not been determined at what precise time this step was taken, but it no doubt long antedates the Norman conquest. It is mentioned by Professor Stubbs as being already, in the reign of Henry III., a custom of immemorial antiquity.[12] It was one of the greatest steps ever taken in the political history of mankind. In these four discreet men we have the forerunners of the two burghers from each town who were summoned by Earl Simon to the famous parliament of 1265, as well as of the two knights from each shire whom the king had summoned eleven years before. In these four discreet men sent to speak for their township in the old county assembly, we have the germ of institutions that have ripened into the House of Commons and into the legislatures of modern kingdoms and republics. In the system of representation thus inaugurated lay the future possibility of such gigantic political aggregates as the United States of America.

In the ancient city, on the other hand, the extreme compactness of the political structure made representation unnecessary and prevented it from being thought of in circumstances where it might have proved of immense value. In an aristocratic Greek city, like Sparta, all the members of the ruling class met together and voted in the assembly; in a democratic city, like Athens, all the free citizens met and voted; in each case the assembly was primary and not representative. The only exception, in all Greek antiquity, is one which emphatically proves the rule. The Amphiktyonic Council, an institution of prehistoric origin, concerned mainly with religious affairs pertaining to the worship of the Delphic Apollo, furnished a precedent for a representative, and indeed for a federal, assembly. Delegates from various Greek tribes and cities attended it. The fact that with such a suggestive precedent before their eyes the Greeks never once hit upon the device of representation, even in their attempts at framing federal unions, shows how thoroughly their whole political training had operated to exclude such a conception from their minds.

The second great consequence of the Graeco-Roman city-system was linked in many ways with this absence of the representative principle. In Greece the formation of political aggregates higher and more extensive than the city was, until a late date, rendered impossible. The good and bad sides of this peculiar phase of civilization have been often enough commented on by historians. On the one hand the democratic assembly of such an imperial city as Athens furnished a school of political training superior to anything else that the world has ever seen. It was something like what the New England town-meeting would be if it were continually required to adjust complicated questions of international polity, if it were carried on in the very centre or point of confluence of all contemporary streams of culture, and if it were in the habit every few days of listening to statesmen and orators like Hamilton or Webster, jurists like Marshall, generals like Sherman, poets like Lowell, historians like Parkman. Nothing in all history has approached the high-wrought intensity and brilliancy of the political life of Athens.

On the other hand, the smallness of the independent city, as a political aggregate, made it of little or no use in diminishing the liability to perpetual warfare which is the curse of all primitive communities. In a group of independent cities, such as made up the Hellenic world, the tendency to warfare is almost as strong, and the occasions for warfare are almost as frequent, as in a congeries of mutually hostile tribes of barbarians. There is something almost lurid in the sharpness of contrast with which the wonderful height of humanity attained by Hellas is set off against the fierce barbarism which characterized the relations of its cities to one another. It may be laid down as a general rule that in an early state of society, where the political aggregations are small, warfare is universal and cruel. From the intensity of the jealousies and rivalries between adjacent self-governing groups of men, nothing short of chronic warfare can result, until some principle of union is evolved by which disputes can be settled in accordance with general principles admitted by all. Among peoples that have never risen above the tribal stage of aggregation, such as the American Indians, war is the normal condition of things, and there is nothing fit to be called peace,--there are only truces of brief and uncertain duration. Were it not for this there would be somewhat less to be said in favour of great states and kingdoms. As modern life grows more and more complicated and interdependent, the Great State subserves innumerable useful purposes; but in the history of civilization its first service, both in order of time and in order of importance, consists in the diminution of the quantity of warfare and in the narrowing of its sphere. For within the territorial limits of any great and permanent state, the tendency is for warfare to become the exception and peace the rule. In this direction the political careers of the Greek cities assisted the progress of civilization but little.

Under the conditions of Graeco-Roman civic life there were but two practicable methods of forming a great state and diminishing the quantity of warfare. The one method was conquest with incorporation, the other method was federation. Either one city might conquer all the others and endow their citizens with its own franchise, or all the cities might give up part of their sovereignty to a federal body which should have power to keep the peace, and should represent the civilized world of the time in its relations with outlying barbaric peoples. Of these two methods, obviously the latter is much the more effective, but it presupposes for its successful adoption a higher general state of civilization than the former. Neither method was adopted by the Greeks in their day of greatness. The Spartan method of extending its power was conquest without incorporation: when Sparta conquered another Greek city, she sent a harmost to govern it like a tyrant; in other words she virtually enslaved the subject city. The efforts of Athens tended more in the direction of a peaceful federalism. In the great Delian confederacy which developed into the maritime empire of Athens, the Aegean cities were treated as allies rather than subjects. As regards their local affairs they were in no way interfered with, and could they have been represented in some kind of a federal council at Athens, the course of Grecian history might have been wonderfully altered. As it was, they were all deprived of one essential element of sovereignty,--the power of controlling their own military forces. Some of them, as Chios and Mitylene, furnished troops at the demand of Athens; others maintained no troops, but paid a fixed tribute to Athens in return for her protection. In either case they felt shorn of part of their dignity, though otherwise they had nothing to complain of; and during the Peloponnesian war Athens had to reckon with their tendency to revolt as well as with her Dorian enemies. Such a confederation was naturally doomed to speedy overthrow.

In the century following the death of Alexander, in the closing age of Hellenic independence, the federal idea appears in a much more advanced stage of elaboration, though in a part of Greece which had been held of little account in the great days of Athens and Sparta. Between the Achaian federation, framed in 274 B.C., and the United States of America, there are some interesting points of resemblance which have been elaborately discussed by Mr. Freeman, in his "History of Federal Government." About the same time the Aetolian League came into prominence in the north. Both these leagues were instances of true federal government, and were not mere confederations; that is, the central government acted directly upon all the citizens and not merely upon the local governments. Each of these leagues had for its chief executive officer a General elected for one year, with powers similar to those of an American President. In each the supreme assembly was a primary assembly at which every citizen from every city of the league had a right to be present, to speak, and to vote; but as a natural consequence these assemblies shrank into comparatively aristocratic bodies. In Aeolia, which was a group of mountain cantons similar to Switzerland, the federal union was more complete than in Achaia, which was a group of cities. In Achaia cases occurred in which a single city was allowed to deal separately with foreign powers. Here, as in earlier Greek history, the instinct of autonomy was too powerful to admit of complete federation. Yet the career of the Achaian League was not an inglorious one. For nearly a century and a half it gave the Peloponnesos a larger measure of orderly government than the country had ever known before, without infringing upon local liberties. It defied successfully the threats and assaults of Macedonia, and yielded at last only to the all-conquering might of Rome.

Thus in so far as Greece contributed anything towards the formation of great and pacific political aggregates, she did it through attempts at federation. But in so low a state of political development as that which prevailed throughout the Mediterranean world in pre-Christian times, the more barbarous method of conquest with incorporation was more likely to be successful on a great scale. This was well illustrated in the history of Rome,--a civic community of the same generic type with Sparta and Athens, but presenting specific differences of the highest importance. The beginnings of Rome, unfortunately, are prehistoric. I have often thought that if some beneficent fairy could grant us the power of somewhere raising the veil of oblivion which enshrouds the earliest ages of Aryan dominion in Europe, there is no place from which the historian should be more glad to see it lifted than from Rome in the centuries which saw the formation of the city, and which preceded the expulsion of the kings. Even the legends, which were uncritically accepted from the days of Livy to those of our grandfathers, are provokingly silent upon the very points as to which we would fain get at least a hint. This much is plain, however, that in the embryonic stage of the Roman commonwealth some obscure processes of fusion or commingling went on. The tribal population of Rome was more heterogeneous than that of the great cities of Greece, and its earliest municipal religion seems to have been an assemblage of various tribal religions that had points of contact with other tribal religions throughout large portions of the Greco-Italic world. As M. de Coulanges observes,[13] Rome was almost the only city of antiquity which was not kept apart from other cities by its religion. There was hardly a people in Greece or Italy which it was restrained from admitting to participation in its municipal rites.

However this may have been, it is certain that Rome early succeeded in freeing itself from that insuperable prejudice which elsewhere prevented the ancient city from admitting aliens to a share in its franchise. And in this victory over primeval political ideas lay the whole secret of Rome's mighty career. The victory was not indeed completed until after the terrible Social War of B.C. 90, but it was begun at least four centuries earlier with the admission of the plebeians. At the consummation of the conquest of Italy in B.C. 270 Roman burghership already extended, in varying degrees of completeness, through the greater part of Etruria and Campania, from the coast to the mountains; while all the rest of Italy was admitted to privileges for which ancient history had elsewhere furnished no precedent. Hence the invasion of Hannibal half a century later, even with its stupendous victories of Thrasymene and Cannae, effected nothing toward detaching the Italian subjects from their allegiance to Rome; and herein we have a most instructive contrast to the conduct of the communities subject to Athens at several critical moments of the Peloponnesian War. With this consolidation of Italy, thus triumphantly demonstrated, the whole problem of the conquering career of Rome was solved. All that came afterwards was simply a corollary from this. The concentration of all the fighting power of the peninsula into the hands of the ruling city formed a stronger political aggregate than anything the world had as yet seen. It was not only proof against the efforts of the greatest military genius of antiquity, but whenever it was brought into conflict with the looser organizations of Greece, Africa, and Asia, or with the semi-barbarous tribes of Spain and Gaul, the result of the struggle was virtually predetermined. The universal dominion of Rome was inevitable, so soon as the political union of Italy had been accomplished. Among the Romans themselves there were those who thoroughly understood this point, as we may see from the interesting speech of the emperor Claudius in favour of admitting Gauls to the senate.

The benefits conferred upon the world by the, universal dominion of Rome were of quite inestimable value. First of these benefits, and (as it were) the material basis of the others, was the prolonged peace that was enforced throughout large portions of the world where chronic warfare had hitherto prevailed. The pax romana has perhaps been sometimes depicted in exaggerated colours; but as compared with all that had preceded, and with all that followed, down to the beginning of the nineteenth century, it deserved the encomiums it has received. The second benefit was the mingling and mutual destruction of the primitive tribal and municipal religions, thus clearing the way for Christianity,--a step which, regarded from a purely political point of view, was of immense importance for the further consolidation of society in Europe. The third benefit was the development of the Roman law into a great body of legal precepts and principles leavened throughout with ethical principles of universal applicability, and the gradual substitution of this Roman law for the innumerable local usages of ancient communities. Thus arose the idea of a common Christendom, of a brotherhood of peoples associated both by common beliefs regarding the unseen world and by common principles of action in the daily affairs of life. The common ethical and traditional basis thus established for the future development of the great nationalities of Europe is the most fundamental characteristic distinguishing modern from ancient history.

While, however, it secured these benefits for mankind for all time to come, the Roman political system in itself was one which could not possibly endure. That extension of the franchise which made Rome's conquests possible, was, after all, the extension of a franchise which could only be practically enjoyed within the walls of the imperial city itself. From first to last the device of representation was never thought of, and from first to last the Roman comitia remained a primary assembly. The result was that, as the burgherhood enlarged, the assembly became a huge mob as little fitted for the transaction of public business as a town-meeting of all the inhabitants of New York would be. The functions which in Athens were performed by the assembly were accordingly in Rome performed largely by the aristocratic senate; and for the conflicts consequently arising between the senatorial and the popular parties it was difficult to find any adequate constitutional check. Outside of Italy, moreover, in the absence of a representative system, the Roman government was a despotism which, whether more or less oppressive, could in the nature of things be nothing else than a despotism. But nothing is more dangerous for a free people than the attempt to govern a dependent people despotically. The bad government kills out the good government as surely as slave-labour destroys free-labour, or as a debased currency drives out a sound currency. The existence of proconsuls in the provinces, with great armies at their beck and call, brought about such results as might have been predicted, as soon as the growing anarchy at home furnished a valid excuse for armed interference. In the case of the Roman world, however, the result is not to be deplored, for it simply substituted a government that was practicable under the circumstances for one that had become demonstrably impracticable.

As regards the provinces the change from senatorial to imperial government at Rome was a great gain, inasmuch as it substituted an orderly and responsible administration for irregular and irresponsible extortion. For a long time, too, it was no part of the imperial policy to interfere with local customs and privileges. But, in the absence of a representative system, the centralizing tendency inseparable from the position of such a government proved to be irresistible. And the strength of this centralizing tendency was further enhanced by the military character of the government which was necessitated by perpetual frontier warfare against the barbarians. As year after year went by, the provincial towns and cities were governed less and less by their local magistrates, more and more by prefects responsible to the emperor only. There were other co-operating causes, economical and social, for the decline of the empire; but this change alone, which was consummated by the time of Diocletian, was quite enough to burn out the candle of Roman strength at both ends. With the decrease in the power of the local governments came an increase in the burdens of taxation and conscription that were laid upon them.[14] And as "the dislocation of commerce and industry caused by the barbarian inroads, and the increasing demands of the central administration for the payment of its countless officials and the maintenance of its troops, all went together," the load at last became greater "than human nature could endure." By the time of the great invasions of the fifth century, local political life had gone far towards extinction throughout Roman Europe, and the tribal organization of the Teutons prevailed in the struggle simply because it had come to be politically stronger than any organization that was left to oppose it.

We have now seen how the two great political systems that were founded upon the Ancient City both ended in failure, though both achieved enormous and lasting results. And we have seen how largely both these political failures were due to the absence of the principle of representation from the public life of Greece and Rome. The chief problem of civilization, from the political point of view, has always been how to secure concerted action among men on a great scale without sacrificing local independence. The ancient history of Europe shows that it is not possible to solve this problem without the aid of the principle of representation. Greece, until overcome by external force, sacredly maintained local self-government, but in securing permanent concert of action it was conspicuously unsuccessful. Rome secured concert of action on a gigantic scale, and transformed the thousand unconnected tribes and cities it conquered into an organized European world, but in doing this it went far towards extinguishing local self-government. The advent of the Teutons upon the scene seems therefore to have been necessary, if only to supply the indispensable element without which the dilemma of civilization could not be surmounted. The turbulence of Europe during the Teutonic migrations was so great and so long continued, that on a superficial view one might be excused for regarding the good work of Rome as largely undone. And in the feudal isolation of effort and apparent incapacity for combined action which characterized the different parts of Europe after the downfall of the Carolingian empire, it might well have seemed that political society had reverted towards a primitive type of structure. In truth, however, the retrogradation was much slighter than appeared on the surface. Feudalism itself, with its curious net-work of fealties and obligations running through the fabric of society in every direction, was by no means purely disintegrative in its tendencies. The mutual relations of rival baronies were by no means like those of rival clans or tribes in pre-Roman days. The central power of Rome, though no longer exerted politically through curators and prefects, was no less effective in the potent hands of the clergy and in the traditions of the imperial jurisprudence by which the legal ideas of mediaeval society were so strongly coloured. So powerful, indeed, was this twofold influence of Rome, that in the later Middle Ages, when the modern nationalities had fairly taken shape, it was the capacity for local self-government--in spite of all the Teutonic reinforcement it had had--that had suffered much more than the capacity for national consolidation. Among the great modern nations it was only England--which in its political development had remained more independent of the Roman law and the Roman church than even the Teutonic fatherland itself--it was only England that came out of the medieval crucible with its Teutonic self-government substantially intact. On the main-land only two little spots, at the two extremities of the old Teutonic world, had fared equally well. At the mouth of the Rhine the little Dutch communities were prepared to lead the attack in the terrible battle for freedom with which the drama of modern history was ushered in. In the impregnable mountain fastnesses of upper Germany the Swiss cantons had bid defiance alike to Austrian tyrant and to Burgundian invader, and had preserved in its purest form the rustic democracy of their Aryan forefathers. By a curious coincidence, both these free peoples, in their efforts towards national unity, were led to frame federal unions, and one of these political achievements is, from the stand-point of universal history, of very great significance. The old League of High Germany, which earned immortal renown at Morgarten and Sempach, consisted of German-speaking cantons only. But in the fifteenth century the League won by force of arms a small bit of Italian territory about Lake Lugano, and in the sixteenth the powerful city of Bern annexed the Burgundian bishopric of Lausanne and rescued the free city of Geneva from the clutches of the Duke of Savoy. Other Burgundian possessions of Savoy were seized by the canton of Freiburg; and after awhile all these subjects and allies were admitted on equal terms into the confederation. The result is that modern Switzerland is made up of what might seem to be most discordant and unmanageable elements. Four languages--German, French, Italian, and Rhaetian--are spoken within the limits of the confederacy; and in point of religion the cantons are sharply divided as Catholic and Protestant. Yet in spite of all this, Switzerland is as thoroughly united in feeling as any nation in Europe. To the German-speaking Catholic of Altdorf the German Catholics of Bavaria are foreigners, while the French-speaking Protestants of Geneva are fellow-countrymen. Deeper down even than these deep-seated differences of speech and creed lies the feeling that comes from the common possession of a political freedom that is greater than that possessed by surrounding peoples. Such has been the happy outcome of the first attempt at federal union made by men of Teutonic descent. Complete independence in local affairs, when combined with adequate representation in the federal council, has effected such an intense cohesion of interests throughout the nation as no centralized government, however cunningly devised, could ever have secured.

Until the nineteenth century, however, the federal form of government had given no clear indication of its capacity for holding together great bodies of men, spread over vast territorial areas, in orderly and peaceful relations with one another. The empire of Trajan and Marcus Aurelius still remained the greatest known example of political aggregation; and men who argued from simple historic precedent without that power of analyzing precedents which the comparative method has supplied, came not unnaturally to the conclusions that great political aggregates have an inherent tendency towards breaking up, and that great political aggregates cannot be maintained except by a strongly- centralized administration and at the sacrifice of local self- government. A century ago the very idea of a stable federation of forty powerful states, covering a territory nearly equal in area to the whole of Europe, carried on by a republican government elected by universal suffrage, and guaranteeing to every tiniest village its full meed of local independence,--the very idea of all this would have been scouted as a thoroughly impracticable Utopian dream. And such scepticism would have been quite justifiable, for European history did not seem to afford any precedents upon which such a forecast of the future could be logically based. Between the various nations of Europe there has certainly always existed an element of political community, bequeathed by the Roman empire, manifested during the Middle Ages in a common relationship to the Church, and in modern times in a common adherence to certain uncodified rules of international law, more or less im perfectly defined and enforced. Between England and Spain, for example, or between France and Austria, there has never been such utter political severance as existed normally between Greece and Persia, or Rome and Carthage. But this community of political inheritance in Europe, it is needless to say, falls very far short of the degree of community implied in a federal union; and so great is the diversity of language and of creed, and of local historic development with the deep-seated prejudices attendant thereupon, that the formation of a European federation could hardly be looked for except as the result of mighty though quiet and subtle influences operating for a long time from without. From what direction, and in what manner, such an irresistible though perfectly pacific pressure is likely to be exerted in the future, I shall endeavour to show in my next lecture. At present we have to observe that the experiment of federal union on a grand scale required as its conditions, first, a vast extent of unoccupied country which could be settled without much warfare by men of the same race and speech, and secondly, on the part of the settlers, a rich inheritance of political training such as is afforded by long ages of self-government. The Atlantic coast of North America, easily accessible to Europe, yet remote enough to be freed from the political complications of the old world, furnished the first of these conditions: the history of the English people through fifty generations furnished the second. It was through English self-government, as I argued in my first lecture, that England alone, among the great nations of Europe, was able to found durable and self-supporting colonies. I have now to add that it was only England, among all the great nations of Europe, that could send forth colonists capable of dealing successfully with the difficult problem of forming such a political aggregate as the United States have become. For obviously the preservation of local self-government is essential to the very idea of a federal union. Without the Town-Meeting, or its equivalent in some form or other, the Federal Union would become ipso facto converted into a centralizing imperial government. Should anything of this sort ever happen--should American towns ever come to be ruled by prefects appointed at Washington, and should American States ever become like the administrative departments of France, or even like the counties of England at the present day--then the time will have come when men may safely predict the break-up of the American political system by reason of its overgrown dimensions and the diversity of interests between its parts. States so unlike one another as Maine and Louisiana and California cannot be held together by the stiff bonds of a centralizing government. The durableness of the federal union lies in its flexibility, and it is this flexibility which makes it the only kind of government, according to modern ideas, that is permanently applicable to a whole continent. If the United States were to-day a consolidated republic like France, recent events in California might have disturbed the peace of the country. But in the federal union, if California, as a state sovereign within its own sphere, adopts a grotesque constitution that aims at infringing on the rights of capitalists, the other states are not directly affected. They may disapprove, but they have neither the right nor the desire to interfere. Meanwhile the laws of nature quietly operate to repair the blunder. Capital flows away from California, and the business of the state is damaged, until presently the ignorant demagogues lose favour, the silly constitution becomes a dead-letter, and its formal repeal begins to be talked of. Not the smallest ripple of excitement disturbs the profound peace of the country at large. It is in this complete independence that is preserved by every state, in all matters save those in which the federal principle itself is concerned, that we find the surest guaranty of the permanence of the American political system. Obviously no race of men, save the race to which habits of self-government and the skilful use of political representation had come to be as second nature, could ever have succeeded in founding such a system.

Yet even by men of English race, working with out let or hindrance from any foreign source, and with the better part of a continent at their disposal for a field to work in, so great a political problem as that of the American Union has not been solved without much toil and trouble. The great puzzle of civilization--how to secure permanent concert of action without sacrificing independence of action--is a puzzle which has taxed the ingenuity of Americans as well as of older Aryan peoples. In the year 1788 when our Federal Union was completed, the problem had already occupied the minds of American statesmen for a century and a half,--that is to say, ever since the English settlement of Massachusetts. In 1643 a New England confederation was formed between Massachusetts and Connecticut, together with Plymouth since merged in Massachusetts and New Haven since merged in Connecticut. The confederation was formed for defence against the French in Canada, the Dutch on the Hudson river, and the Indians. But owing simply to the inequality in the sizes of these colonies--Massachusetts more than outweighing the other three combined--the practical working of this confederacy was never very successful. In 1754, just before the outbreak of the great war which drove the French from America, a general Congress of the colonies was held at Albany, and a comprehensive scheme of union was proposed by Benjamin Franklin, but nothing came of the project at that time. The commercial rivalry between the colonies, and their disputes over boundary lines, were then quite like the similar phenomena with which Europe had so long been familiar. In 1756 Georgia and South Carolina actually came to blows over the navigation of the Savannah river. The idea that the thirteen colonies could ever overcome their mutual jealousies so far as to unite in a single political body, was received at that time in England with a derision like that which a proposal for a permanent federation of European States would excite in many minds to-day. It was confidently predicted that if the common allegiance to the British crown were once withdrawn, the colonies would forthwith proceed to destroy themselves with internecine war. In fact, however, it was the shaking off of allegiance to the British crown, and the common trials and sufferings of the war of independence, that at last welded the colonies together and made a federal union possible. As it was, the union was consummated only by degrees. By the Articles of Confederation, agreed on by Congress in 1777 but not adopted by all the States until 1781, the federal government acted only upon the several state governments and not directly upon individuals; there was no federal judiciary for the decision of constitutional questions arising out of the relations between the states; and the Congress was not provided with any efficient means of raising a revenue or of enforcing its legislative decrees. Under such a government the difficulty of insuring concerted action was so great that, but for the transcendent personal qualities of Washington, the bungling mismanagement of the British ministry, and the timely aid of the French fleet, the war of independence would most likely have ended in failure. After the independence of the colonies was acknowledged, the formation of a more perfect union was seen to be the only method of securing peace and making a nation which should be respected by foreign powers; and so in 1788, after much discussion, the present Constitution of the United States was adopted,--a constitution which satisfied very few people at the time, and which was from beginning to end a series of compromises, yet which has proved in its working a masterpiece of political wisdom.

The first great compromise answered to the initial difficulty of securing approximate equality of weight in the federal councils between states of unequal size. The simple device by which this difficulty was at last surmounted has proved effectual, although the inequalities between the states have greatly increased. To-day the population of New York is more than eighty times that of Nevada. In area the state of Rhode Island is smaller than Montenegro, while the state of Texas is larger than the Austrian empire with Bavaria and Westemberg thrown in. Yet New York and Nevada, Rhode Island and Texas, each send two senators to Washington, while on the other hand in the lower house each state has a number of representatives proportioned to its population. The upper house of Congress is therefore a federal while the lower house is a national body, and the government is brought into direct contact with the people without endangering the equal rights of the several states.

The second great compromise of the American constitution consists in the series of arrangements by which sovereignty is divided between the states and the federal government. In all domestic legislation and jurisdiction, civil and criminal, in all matters relating to tenure of property, marriage and divorce, the fulfilment of contracts and the punishment of malefactors, each separate state is as completely a sovereign state as France or Great Britain. In speaking to a British audience a concrete illustration may not be superfluous. If a criminal is condemned to death in Pennsylvania, the royal prerogative of pardon resides in the Governor of Pennsylvania: the President of the United States has no more authority in the case than the Czar of Russia. Nor in civil cases can an appeal lie from the state courts to the Supreme Court of the United States, save where express provision has been made in the Constitution. Within its own sphere the state is supreme. The chief attributes of sovereignty with which the several states have parted are the coining of money, the carrying of mails, the imposition of tariff dues, the granting of patents and copyrights, the declaration of war, and the maintenance of a navy. The regular army is supported and controlled by the federal government, but each state maintains its own militia which it is bound to use in case of internal disturbance before calling upon the central government for aid. In time of war, however, these militias come under the control of the central government. Thus every American citizen lives under two governments, the functions of which are clearly and intelligibly distinct.

To insure the stability of the federal union thus formed, the Constitution created a "system of United States courts extending throughout the states, empowered to define the boundaries of federal authority, and to enforce its decisions by federal power." This omnipresent federal judiciary was undoubtedly the most important creation of the statesmen who framed the Constitution. The closely-knit relations which it established between the states contributed powerfully to the growth of a feeling of national solidarity throughout the whole country. The United States today cling together with a coherency far greater than the coherency of any ordinary federation or league. Yet the primary aspect of the federal Constitution was undoubtedly that of a permanent league, in which each state, while retaining its domestic sovereignty intact, renounced forever its right to make war upon its neighbours and relegated its international interests to the care of a central council in which all the states were alike represented and a central tribunal endowed with purely judicial functions of interpretation. It was the first attempt in the history of the world, to apply on a grand scale to the relations between states the same legal methods of procedure which, as long applied in all civilized countries to the relations between individuals, have rendered private warfare obsolete. And it was so far successful that, during a period of seventy-two years in which the United States increased fourfold in extent, tenfold in population, and more than tenfold in wealth and power, the federal union maintained a state of peace more profound than the _pax romana._

Twenty years ago this unexampled state of peace was suddenly interrupted by a tremendous war, which in its results, however, has served only to bring out with fresh emphasis the pacific implications of federalism. With the eleven revolted states at first completely conquered and then reinstated with full rights and privileges in the federal union, with their people accepting in good faith the results of the contest, with their leaders not executed as traitors but admitted again to seats in Congress and in the Cabinet, and with all this accomplished without any violent constitutional changes,--I think we may fairly claim that the strength of the pacific implications of federalism has been more strikingly demonstrated than if there had been no war at all. Certainly the world never beheld such a spectacle before. In my next and concluding lecture I shall return to this point while summing up the argument and illustrating the part played by the English race in the general history of civilization.

III.

"MANIFEST DESTINY."

Among the legends of our late Civil War there is a story of a dinner-party given by the Americans residing in Paris, at which were propounded sundry toasts concerning not so much the past and present as the expected glories of the great American nation. In the general character of these toasts geographical considerations were very prominent, and the principal fact which seemed to occupy the minds of the speakers was the unprecedented bigness of our country. "Here's to the United States," said the first speaker, "bounded on the north by British America, on the south by the Gulf of Mexico, on the east by the Atlantic, and on the west by the Pacific, Ocean." "But," said the second speaker, "this is far too limited a view of the subject: in assigning our boundaries we must look to the great and glorious future which is prescribed for us by the Manifest Destiny of the Anglo-Saxon Race. Here's to the United States,--bounded on the north by the North Pole, on the south by the South Pole, on the east by the rising and on the west by the setting sun." Emphatic applause greeted this aspiring prophecy. But here arose the third speaker--a very serious gentleman from the Far West. "If we are going," said this truly patriotic American, "to leave the historic past and present, and take our manifest destiny into the account, why restrict ourselves within the narrow limits assigned by our fellow-countryman who has just sat down? I give you the United States,--bounded on the north by the Aurora Borealis, on the south by the precession of the equinoxes, on the east by the primeval chaos, and on the west by the Day of Judgment!"

I offer this anecdote at the outset by way of self-defence, inasmuch as I shall by and by have myself to introduce some considerations concerning the future of our country, and of what some people, without the fear of Mr. Freeman before their eyes, call the "Anglo-Saxon" race; and if it should happen to strike you that my calculations are unreasonably large, I hope you will remember that they are quite modest after all, when compared with some others.

The "manifest destiny" of the "Anglo-Saxon" race and the huge dimensions of our country are favourite topics with Fourth-of-July orators, but they are none the less interesting on that account when considered from the point of view of the historian. To be a citizen of a great and growing state, or to belong to one of the dominant races of the world, is no doubt a legitimate source of patriotic pride, though there is perhaps an equal justification for such a feeling in being a citizen of a tiny state like Holland, which, in spite of its small dimensions, has nevertheless achieved so much,--fighting at one time the battle of freedom for the world, producing statesmen like William and Barneveldt, generals like Maurice, scholars like Erasmus and Grotius, and thinkers like Spinoza, and taking the lead even to-day in the study of Christianity and in the interpretation of the Bible. But my course in the present lecture is determined by historical or philosophical rather than by patriotic interest, and I shall endeavour to characterize and group events as impartially as if my home were at Leyden in the Old World instead of Cambridge in the New.

First of all, I shall take sides with Mr. Freeman in eschewing altogether the word "Anglo-Saxon." The term is sufficiently absurd and misleading as applied in England to the Old-English speech of our forefathers, or to that portion of English history which is included between the fifth and the eleventh centuries. But in America it is frequently used, not indeed by scholars, but by popular writers and speakers, in a still more loose and slovenly way. In the war of independence our great-great-grandfathers, not yet having ceased to think of themselves as Englishmen, used to distinguish themselves as "Continentals," while the king's troops were known as the "British." The quaint term "Continental" long ago fell into disuse, except in the slang phrase "not worth a Continental" which referred to the debased condition of our currency at the close of the Revolutionary War; but "American" and "British" might still serve the purpose sufficiently whenever it is necessary to distinguish between the two great English nationalities. The term "English," however, is so often used with sole reference to people and things in England as to have become in some measure antithetical to "American;" and when it is found desirable to include the two in a general expression, one often hears in America the term "Anglo-Saxon" colloquially employed for this purpose. A more slovenly use of language can hardly be imagined. Such a compound term as "Anglo-American" might perhaps be logically defensible, but that has already become restricted to the English-descended inhabitants of the United States and Canada alone, in distinction from Spanish Americans and red Indians. It is never so used as to include Englishmen. Refraining from all such barbarisms, I prefer to call the English race by the name which it has always applied to itself, from the time when it inhabited the little district of Angeln on the Baltic coast of Sleswick down to the time when it had begun to spread itself over three great continents. It is a race which has shown a rare capacity for absorbing slightly foreign elements and moulding them into conformity with a political type that was first wrought out through centuries of effort on British soil; and this capacity it has shown perhaps in a heightened degree in the peculiar circumstances in which it has been placed in America. The American has absorbed considerable quantities of closely kindred European blood, but he is rapidly assimilating it all, and in his political habits and aptitudes he remains as thoroughly English as his forefathers in the days of De Montfort, or Hampden, or Washington. Premising this, we may go on to consider some aspects of the work which the English race has done and is doing in the world, and we need not feel discouraged if, in order to do justice to the subject, we have to take our start far back in ancient history. We shall begin, it may be said, somewhere near the primeval chaos, and though we shall indeed stop short of the day of judgment, we shall hope at all events to reach the millennium.

Our eloquent friends of the Paris dinner-party seem to have been strongly impressed with the excellence of enormous political aggregates. We, too, approaching the subject from a different point of view, have been led to see how desirable it is that self-governing groups of men should be enabled to work together in permanent harmony and on a great scale. In this kind of political integration the work of civilization very largely consists. We have seen how in its most primitive form political society is made up of small self-governing groups that are perpetually at war with one another. Now the process of change which we call civilization means quite a number of things. But there is no doubt that on its political side it means primarily the gradual substitution of a state of peace for a state of war. This change is the condition precedent for all the other kinds of improvement that are connoted by such a term as "civilization." Manifestly the development of industry is largely dependent upon the cessation or restriction of warfare; and furthermore, as the industrial phase of civilization slowly supplants the military phase, men's characters undergo, though very slowly, a corresponding change. Men become less inclined to destroy life or to inflict pain; or--to use the popular terminology which happens here to coincide precisely with that of the Doctrine of Evolution--they become less brutal and more humane. Obviously then the prime feature of the process called civilization is the general diminution of warfare. But we have seen that a general diminution of warfare is rendered possible only by the union of small political groups into larger groups that are kept together by community of interests, and that can adjust their mutual relations by legal discussion without coming to blows. In the preceding lecture we considered this process of political integration as variously exemplified by communities of Hellenic, of Roman, and of Teutonic race, and we saw how manifold were the difficulties which the process had to encounter. We saw how the Teutons--at least in Switzerland, England, and America--had succeeded best through the retention of local self-government combined with central representation. We saw how the Romans failed of ultimate success because by weakening self-government they weakened that community of interest which is essential to the permanence of a great political aggregate. We saw how the Greeks, after passing through their most glorious period in a state of chronic warfare, had begun to achieve considerable success in forming a pacific federation when their independent career was suddenly cut short by the Roman conqueror.

This last example introduces us to a fresh consideration, of very great importance. It is not only that every progressive community has had to solve, in one way or another, the problem of securing permanent concert of action without sacrificing local independence of action; but while engaged in this difficult work the community has had to defend itself against the attacks of other communities. In the case just cited, of the conquest of Greece by Rome, little harm was done perhaps. But under different circumstances immense damage may have been done in this way, and the nearer we go to the beginnings of civilization the greater the danger. At the dawn of history we see a few brilliant points of civilization surrounded on every side by a midnight blackness of barbarism. In order that the pacific community may be able to go on doing its work, it must be strong enough and warlike enough to overcome its barbaric neighbours who have no notion whatever of keeping peace. This is another of the seeming paradoxes of the history of civilization, that for a very long time the possibility of peace can be guaranteed only through war. Obviously the permanent peace of the world can be secured only through the gradual concentration of the preponderant military strength into the hands of the most pacific communities. With infinite toil and trouble this point has been slowly gained by mankind, through the circumstance that the very same political aggregation of small primitive communities which makes them less disposed to quarrel among themselves tends also to make them more than a match for the less coherent groups of their more barbarous neighbours. The same concert of action which tends towards internal harmony tends also towards external victory, and both ends are promoted by the co-operation of the same sets of causes. But for a long time all the political problems of the civilized world were complicated by the fact that the community had to fight for its life. We seldom stop to reflect upon the imminent danger from outside attacks, whether from surrounding barbarism or from neighbouring civilizations of lower type, amid which the rich and high-toned civilizations of Greece and Rome were developed. When the king of Persia undertook to reduce Greece to the condition of a Persian satrapy, there was imminent danger that all the enormous fruition of Greek thought in the intellectual life of the European world might have been nipped in the bud. And who can tell how often, in prehistoric times, some little gleam of civilization, less bright and steady than this one had become, may have been quenched in slavery or massacre? The greatest work which the Romans performed in the world was to assume the aggressive against menacing barbarism, to subdue it, to tame it, and to enlist its brute force on the side of law and order. This was a murderous work, and in doing it the Romans became excessively cruel, but it had to be done by some one before you could expect to have great and peaceful civilizations like our own. The warfare of Rome is by no means adequately explained by the theory of a deliberate immoral policy of aggression,--"infernal," I believe, is the stronger adjective which Dr. Draper uses. The aggressive wars of Rome were largely dictated by just such considerations as those which a century ago made it necessary for the English to put down the raids of the Scotch Highlanders, and which have since made it necessary for Russia to subdue the Caucasus. It is not easy for a turbulent community to live next to an orderly one without continually stirring up frontier disturbances which call for stern repression from the orderly community. Such considerations go far towards explaining the military history of the Romans, and it is a history with which, on the whole, we ought to sympathize. In its European relations that history is the history of the moving of the civilized frontier northward and eastward against the disastrous encroachments of barbarous peoples. This great movement has, on the whole, been steadily kept up, in spite of some apparent fluctuation in the fifth and sixth centuries of the Christian era, and it is still going on to-day. It was a great gain for civilization when the Romans overcame the Keltiberians of Spain, and taught them good manners and the Latin language, and made it for their interest hereafter to fight against barbarians. The third European peninsula was thus won over to the side of law and order. Danger now remained on the north. The Gauls had once sacked the city of Rome; hordes of Teutons had lately menaced the very heart of civilization, but had been overthrown in murderous combat by Caius Marius; another great Teutonic movement, led by Ariovistus, now threatened to precipitate the whole barbaric force of south-eastern Gaul upon the civilized world; and so it occurred to the prescient genius of Caesar to be beforehand and conquer Gaul, and enlist all its giant barbaric force on the side of civilization. This great work was as thoroughly done as anything that was ever done in human history, and we ought to be thankful to Caesar for it every day that we live. The frontier to be defended against barbarism was now moved away up to the Rhine, and was very much shortened; but above all, the Gauls were made to feel themselves to be Romans. Their country became one of the chief strongholds of civilization and of Christianity; and when the frightful shock of barbarism came--the most formidable blow that has ever been directed by barbaric brute force against European civilization-- it was in Gaul that it was repelled and that its force was spent. At the beginning of the fifth century an enormous horde of yellow Mongolians, known as Huns, poured down into Europe with avowed intent to burn and destroy all the good work which Rome had wrought in the world; and terrible was the havoc they effected in the course of fifty years. If Attila had carried his point, it has been thought that the work of European civilization might have had to be begun over again. But near Chons-on-the-Marne, in the year

451, in one of the most obstinate struggles of which history preserves the record, the career of the "Scourge of God" was arrested, and mainly by the prowess of Gauls and of Visigoths whom the genius of Rome had tamed. That was the last day on which barbarism was able to contend with civilization on equal terms. It was no doubt a critical day for all future history; and for its favourable issue we must largely thank the policy adopted by Caesar five centuries before. By the end of the eighth century the great power of the Franks had become enlisted in behalf of law and order, and the Roman throne was occupied by a Frank,--the ablest man who had appeared in the world since Caesar's death; and one of the worthiest achievements of Charles the Great was the conquest and conversion of pagan Germany, which threw the frontier against barbarism eastward as far as the Oder, and made it so much the easier to defend Europe. In the thirteenth century this frontier was permanently carried forward to the Vistula by the Teutonic Knights who, under commission from the emperor Frederick II., overcame the heathen Prussians and Lithuanians; and now it began to be shown how greatly the military strength of Europe had increased. In this same century Batu, the grandson of Jinghis Khan, came down into Europe with a horde of more than a million Mongols, and tried to repeat the experiment of Attila. Batu penetrated as far as Silesia, and won a great battle at Liegnitz in 1241, but in spite of his victory he had to desist from the task of conquering Europe. Since the fifth century the physical power of the civilized world had grown immensely; and the impetus of this barbaric invasion was mainly spent upon Russia, the growth of which it succeeded in retarding for more than two centuries. Finally since the sixteenth century we have seen the Russians, redeemed from their Mongolian oppressors, and rich in many of the elements of a vigorous national life,--we have seen the Russians resume the aggressive in this conflict of ages, beginning to do for Central Asia in some sort what the Romans did for Europe. The frontier against barbarism, which Caesar left at the Rhine, has been carried eastward to the Volga, and is now advancing even to the Oxus. The question has sometimes been raised whether it would be possible for European civilization to be seriously threatened by any future invasion of barbarism or of some lower type of civilization. By barbarism certainly not: all the nomad strength of Mongolian

Asia would throw itself in vain against the insuperable barrier constituted by Russia. But I have heard it quite seriously suggested that if some future Attila or Jinghis were to wield as a unit the entire military strength of the four hundred millions of Chinese, possessed with some suddenly-conceived idea of conquering the world, even as Omar and Abderrahman wielded as a unit the newly-welded power of the Saracens in the seventh and eighth centuries, then perhaps a staggering blow might yet be dealt against European civilization. I will not waste precious time in considering this imaginary case, further than to remark that if the Chinese are ever going to try anything of this sort, they cannot afford to wait very long; for within another century, as we shall presently see, their very numbers will be surpassed by those of the English race alone. By that time all the elements of military predominance on the earth, including that of simple numerical superiority, will have been gathered into the hands not merely of men of European descent in general, but more specifically into the hands of the offspring of the Teutonic tribes who conquered Britain in the fifth century. So far as the relations of civilization with barbarism are concerned to-day, the only serious question is by what process of modification the barbarous races are to maintain their foothold upon the earth at all. While once such people threatened the very continuance of civilization, they now exist only on sufferance.

In this brief survey of the advancing frontier of European civilization, I have said nothing about the danger that has from time to time been threatened by the followers of Mohammed,--of the overthrow of the Saracens in Gaul by the grandfather of Charles the Great, or their overthrow at Constantinople by the image-breaking Leo, of the great medieval Crusades, or of the mischievous but futile career of the Turks. For if I were to attempt to draw this outline with anything like completeness, I should have no room left for the conclusion of my argument. Considering my position thus far as sufficiently illustrated, let us go on to contemplate for a moment some of the effects of all this secular turmoil upon the political development of the progressive nations of Europe. I think we may safely lay it down, as a large and general rule, that all this prodigious warfare required to free the civilized world from peril of barbarian attack served greatly to increase the difficulty of solving the great initial problem of civilization. In the first place, the turbulence thus arising was a serious obstacle to the formation of closely-coherent political aggregates; as we see exemplified in the terrible convulsions of the fifth and sixth centuries, and again in the ascendency acquired by the isolating features of feudalism between the time of Charles the Great and the time of Louis VI. of France. In the second place, this perpetual turbulence was a serious obstacle to the preservation of popular liberties. It is a very difficult thing for a free people to maintain its free, constitution if it has to keep perpetually fighting for its life. The "one-man-power." less fit for, carrying on the peaceful pursuits of life, is sure to be brought into the foreground in a state of endless warfare. It is a still more difficult thing for a free people to maintain its free constitution when it undertakes to govern a dependent people despotically, as has been wont to happen when a portion of the barbaric world has been overcome and annexed to the civilized world. Under the weight, of these two difficulties combined, the free institutions of the ancient Romans succumbed, and their government gradually passed into the hands of a kind of close corporation more despotic than anything else of the sort that Europe has ever seen. This despotic character--this tendency, if you will pardon the phrase, towards the Asiaticization of European life--was continued by inheritance in the Roman Church, the influence of which was beneficent so long as it constituted a wholesome check to the isolating tendencies of feudalism, but began to become noxious the moment these tendencies yielded to the centralizing monarchical tendency in nearly all parts of Europe. The asiaticizing tendency of Roman political life had become so powerful by the fourth century, and has since been so powerfully propagated through the Church, that we ought to be glad that the Teutons came into the empire as masters rather than as subjects. As the Germanic tribes got possession of the government in one part of Europe after another, they brought with them free institutions again. The political ideas of the Goths in Spain, of the Lombards in Italy, and of the Franks and Burgundians in Gaul, were as distinctly free as those of the Angles in Britain. But as the outcome of the long and uninterrupted turmoil of the Middle Ages, society throughout the continent of Europe remained predominantly military in type, and this fact greatly increased the tendency towards despotism which was bequeathed by Rome. After the close of the thirteenth century the whole power of the Church was finally thrown into the scale against the liberties of the people; and as the result of all these forces combined, we find that at the time when America was discovered government was hardening into despotism in all the great countries of Europe except England. Even in England the tendency towards despotism had begun to become quite conspicuous after the wholesale slaughter of the great barons and the confiscation of their estates which took place in the Wars of the Roses. The constitutional history of England during the Tudor and Stuart periods is mainly the history of the persistent effort of the English sovereign to free himself from constitutional checks, as his brother sovereigns on the continent were doing. But how different the result! How enormous the political difference between William III. and Louis XIV., compared with the difference between Henry VIII. and Francis I.! The close of the seventeenth century, which marks the culmination of the asiaticizing tendency in Europe, saw despotism both political and religious firmly established in France and Spain and Italy, and in half of Germany; while the rest of Germany seemed to have exhausted itself in the attempt to throw off the incubus. But in England this same epoch saw freedom both political and religious established on so firm a foundation as never again to be shaken, never again with impunity to be threatened, so long as the language of Locke and Milton and Sydney shall remain a living speech on the lips of men. Now this wonderful difference between the career of popular liberty in England and on the Continent was due no doubt to a complicated variety of causes, one or two of which I have already sought to point out. In my first lecture I alluded to the curious combination of circumstances which prevented anything like a severance of interests between the upper and the lower ranks of society; and something was also said about the feebleness of the grasp of imperial Rome upon Britain compared with its grasp upon the continent of Europe. But what I wish now to point out--since we are looking at the military aspect of the subject--is the enormous advantage of what we may call the strategic position of England in the long medieval struggle between civilization and barbarism. In Professor Stubbs's admirable collection of charters and documents illustrative of English history, we read that "on the

6th of July [1264] the whole force of the country was summoned to London for the 3d of August, to resist the army which was coming from France under the queen and her son Edmund. The invading fleet was prevented by the weather from sailing until too late in the season.... The papal legate, Guy Foulquois, who soon after became Clement IV., threatened the barons with excommunication, but the bull containing the sentence was taken by the men of Dover as soon as it arrived, and was thrown into the sea." [15] As I read this, I think of the sturdy men of Connecticut, beating the drum to prevent the reading of the royal order of James II. depriving the colony of the control of its own militia, and feel with pride that the indomitable spirit of English liberty is alike indomitable in every land where men of English race have set their feet as masters. But as the success of Americans in withstanding the unconstitutional pretensions of the crown was greatly favoured by the barrier of the ocean, so the success of Englishmen in defying the enemies of their freedom has no doubt been greatly favoured by the barrier of the British channel. The war between Henry III. and the barons was an event in English history no less critical than the war between Charles I. and the parliament four centuries later; and British and Americans alike have every reason to be thankful that a great French army was not able to get across the channel in August, 1264. Nor was this the only time when the insular position of England did goodly service in maintaining its liberties and its internal peace. We cannot forget how Lord Howard of Effingham, aided also by the weather, defeated the armada that boasted itself "invincible," sent to strangle freedom in its chosen home by the most execrable and ruthless tyrant that Europe has ever seen, a tyrant whose victory would have meant not simply the usurpation of the English crown but the establishment of the Spanish Inquisition at Westminster Hall. Nor can we forget with what longing eyes the Corsican barbarian who wielded for mischief the forces of France in 1805 looked across from Boulogne at the shores of the one European land that never in word or deed granted him homage. But in these latter days England has had no need of stormy weather to aid the prowess of the sea-kings who are her natural defenders. It is impossible for the thoughtful student of history to walk across Trafalgar Square, and gaze on the image of the mightiest naval hero that ever lived, on the summit of his lofty column and guarded by the royal lions, looking down towards the government-house of the land that he freed from the dread of Napoleonic invasion and towards that ancient church wherein the most sacred memories of English talent and English toil are clustered together,--it is impossible, I say, to look at this, and not admire both the artistic instinct that devised so happy a symbolism, and the rare good-fortune of our Teutonic ancestors in securing a territorial position so readily defensible against the assaults of despotic powers. But it was not merely in the simple facility of warding off external attack that the insular position of England was so serviceable. This ease in warding off external attack had its most marked effect upon the internal polity of the nation. It never became necessary for the English government to keep up a great standing army. For purposes of external defence a navy was all-sufficient; and there is this practical difference between a permanent army and a permanent navy. Both are originally designed for purposes of external defence; but the one can readily be used for purposes of internal oppression, and the other cannot. Nobody ever heard of a navy putting up an empire at auction and knocking down the throne of the world to a Didius Julianus. When, therefore, a country is effectually screened by water from external attack, it is screened in a way that permits its normal political development to go on internally without those manifold military hinderances that have ordinarily been so obstructive in the history of civilization. Hence we not only see why, after the Norman Conquest had operated to increase its unity and its strength, England enjoyed a far greater amount of security and was far more peaceful than any other country in Europe; but we also see why society never assumed the military type in England which it assumed upon the continent; we see how it was that the bonds of feudalism were far looser here than elsewhere, and therefore how it happened that nowhere else was the condition of the common people so good politically. We now begin to see, moreover, how thoroughly Professor Stubbs and Mr. Freeman are justified in insisting upon the fact that the political institutions of the Germans of Tacitus have had a more normal and uninterrupted development in England than anywhere else. Nowhere, indeed, in the whole history of the human race, can we point to such a well-rounded and unbroken continuity of political life as we find in the thousand years of English history that have elapsed since the victory of William the Norman at Senlac. In England the free government of the primitive Aryans has been to this day uninterruptedly maintained, though everywhere lost or seriously impaired on the continent of Europe, except in remote Scandinavia and impregnable Switzerland. But obviously, if in the conflict of ages between civilization and barbarism England had occupied such an inferior strategic position as that occupied by Hungary or Poland or Spain, if her territory had been liable once or twice in a century to be overrun by fanatical Saracens or beastly Mongols, no such remarkable and quite exceptional result could have been achieved. Having duly fathomed the significance of this strategic position of the English race while confined within the limits of the British islands, we are now prepared to consider the significance of the stupendous expansion of the English race which first became possible through the discovery and settlement of North America. I said, at the close of my first lecture, that the victory of Wolfe at Quebec marks the greatest turning-point as yet discernible in all modern history. At the first blush such an unqualified statement may have sounded as if an American student of history were inclined to attach an undue value to events that have happened upon his own soil. After the survey of universal history which we have now taken, however, I am fully prepared to show that the conquest of the North American continent by men of English race was unquestionably the most prodigious event in the political annals of man kind. Let us consider, for a moment, the cardinal facts which this English conquest and settlement of North America involved.

Chronologically the discovery of America coincides precisely with the close of the Middle Ages, and with the opening of the drama of what is called modern history. The coincidence is in many ways significant. The close of the Middle Ages--as we have seen--was characterized by the increasing power of the crown in all the great countries of Europe, and by strong symptoms of popular restlessness in view of this increasing power. It was characterized also by the great Protestant outbreak against the despotic pretensions of the Church, which once, in its antagonism to the rival temporal power, had befriended the liberties of the people, but now (especially since the death of Boniface VIII.) sought to enthrall them with a tyranny far worse than that of irresponsible king or emperor. As we have seen Aryan civilization in Europe struggling for many centuries to prove itself superior to the assaults of outer barbarism, so here we find a decisive struggle beginning between the antagonist tendencies which had grown up in the midst of this civilization. Having at length won the privilege of living without risk of slaughter and pillage at the hands of Saracens or Mongols, the question now arose whether the people of Europe should go on and apply their intelligence freely to the problem of making life as rich and fruitful as possible in varied material and spiritual achievement, or should fall forever into the barren and monotonous way of living and thinking which has always distinguished the half-civilized populations of Asia. This--and nothing less than this, I think--was the practical political question really at stake in the sixteenth century between Protestantism and Catholicism. Holland and England entered the lists in behalf of the one solution of this question, while Spain and the Pope defended the other, and the issue was fought out on European soil, as we have seen, with varying success. But the discovery of America now came to open up an enormous region in which whatever seed of civilization should be planted was sure to grow to such enormous dimensions as by and by to exert a controlling influence upon all such controversies. It was for Spain, France, and England to contend for the possession of this vast region, and to prove by the result of the struggle which kind of civilization was endowed with the higher and sturdier political life. The race which here should gain the victory was clearly destined hereafter to take the lead in the world, though the rival powers could not in those days fully appreciate this fact. They who founded colonies in America as trading-stations or military outposts probably did not foresee that these colonies must by and by become imperial states far greater in physical mass than the states which planted them. It is not likely that they were philosophers enough to foresee that this prodigious physical development would mean that the political ideas of the parent state should acquire a hundred-fold power and seminal influence in the future work of the world. It was not until the American Resolution that this began to be dimly realized by a few prescient thinkers. It is by no means so fully realized even now that a clear and thorough-going statement of it has not somewhat an air of novelty. When the highly-civilized community, representing the ripest political ideas of England, was planted in America, removed from the manifold and complicated checks we have just been studying in the history of the Old World, the growth was portentously rapid and steady. There were no Attilas now to stand in the way,--only a Philip or a Pontiac. The assaults of barbarism constituted only a petty annoyance as compared with the conflict of ages which had gone on in Europe. There was no occasion for society to assume a military aspect. Principles of self-government were at once put into operation, and no one thought of calling them in question. When the neighbouring civilization of inferior type--I allude to the French in Canada-- began to become seriously troublesome, it was struck down at a blow. When the mother-country, under the guidance of an ignorant king and short- sighted ministers, undertook to act upon the antiquated theory that the new communities were merely groups of trading-stations, the political bond of connection was severed; yet the war which ensued was not like the war which had but just now been so gloriously ended by the victory of Wolfe. It was not a struggle between two different peoples, like the French of the Old Regime and the English, each representing antagonistic theories of how political life ought to be conducted. But, like the Barons' War of the thirteenth century and the Parliament's War of the seventeenth, it was a struggle sustained by a part of the English people in behalf of principles that time has shown to be equally dear to all. And so the issue only made it apparent to an astonished world that instead of one there were now two Englands, alike prepared to work with might and main toward the political regeneration of mankind.

Let us consider now to what conclusions the rapidity and unabated steadiness of the increase of the English race in America must lead us as we go on to forecast the future. Carlyle somewhere speaks slightingly of the fact that the Americans double their numbers every twenty years, as if to have forty million dollar-hunters in the world were any better than to have twenty million dollar-hunters! The implication that Americans are nothing but dollar- hunters, and are thereby distinguishable from the rest of mankind, would not perhaps bear too elaborate scrutiny. But during the present lecture we have been considering the gradual transfer of the preponderance of physical strength from the hands of the war-loving portion of the human race into the hands of the peace-loving portion,--into the hands of the dollar-hunters, if you please, but out of the hands of the scalp-hunters. Obviously to double the numbers of a pre-eminently industrious, peaceful, orderly, and free-thinking community, is somewhat to increase the weight in the world of the tendencies that go towards making communities free and orderly and peaceful and industrious. So that, from this point of view, the fact we are speaking of is well worth considering, even for its physical dimensions. I do not know whether the United States could support a population everywhere as dense as that of Belgium; so I will suppose that, with ordinary improvement in cultivation and in the industrial arts, we might support a population half as dense as that of Belgium,--and this is no doubt an extremely moderate supposition. Now a very simple operation in arithmetic will show that this means a population of fifteen hundred millions, or more than the population of the whole world at the present date. Another very simple operation in arithmetic will show that if we were to go on doubling our numbers, even once in every twenty-five years, we should reach that stupendous figure at about the close of the twentieth century,--that is, in the days of our great-greatgrandchildren. I do not predict any such result, for there are discernible economic reasons for believing that there will be a diminution in the rate of increase. The rate must nevertheless continue to be very great, in the absence of such causes as formerly retarded the growth of population in Europe. Our modern wars are hideous enough, no doubt, but they are short. They are settled with a few heavy blows, and the loss of life and property occasioned by them is but trifling when compared with the awful ruin and desolation wrought by the perpetual and protracted contests of antiquity and of the Middle Ages. Chronic warfare, both private and public, periodic famines, and sweeping pestilences like the Black Death,--these were the things which formerly shortened human life and kept down population. In the absence of such causes, and with the abundant capacity of our country for feeding its people, I think it an extremely moderate statement if we say that by the end of the next century the English race in the United States will number at least six or seven hundred millions.

It used to be said that so huge a people as this could not be kept together as a single national aggregate,--or, if kept together at all, could only be so by means of a powerful centralized government, like that of ancient Rome under the emperors. I think we are now prepared to see that this is a great mistake. If the Roman Empire could have possessed that political vitality in all its parts which is secured to the United States by the principles of equal representation and of limited state sovereignty, it might well have defied all the shocks which tribally-organized barbarism could ever have directed against it. As it was, its strong centralized government did not save it from political disintegration. One of its weakest political features was precisely this,--that its "strong centralized government" was a kind of close corporation, governing a score of provinces in its own interest rather than in the interest of the provincials. In contrast with such a system as that of the Roman Empire, the skilfully elaborated American system of federalism appears as one of the most important contributions that the English race has made to the general work of civilization. The working out of this feature in our national constitution, by Hamilton and Madison and their associates, was the finest specimen of constructive statesmanship that the world has ever seen. Not that these statesmen originated the principle, but they gave form and expression to the principle which was latent in the circumstances under which the group of American colonies had grown up, and which suggested itself so forcibly that the clear vision of these thinkers did not fail to seize upon it as the fundamental principle upon which alone could the affairs of a great people, spreading over a vast continent, be kept in a condition approaching to something like permanent peace. Stated broadly, so as to acquire somewhat the force of a universal proposition, the principle of federalism is just this:--that the people of a state shall have full and entire control of their own domestic affairs, which directly concern them only, and which they will naturally manage with more intelligence and with more zeal than any distant governing body could possibly exercise; but that, as regards matters of common concern between a group of states, a decision shall in every case be reached, not by brutal warfare or by weary diplomacy, but by the systematic legislation of a central government which represents both states and people, and whose decisions can always be enforced, if necessary, by the combined physical power of all the states. This principle, in various practical applications, is so familiar to Americans to-day that we seldom pause to admire it, any more than we stop to admire the air which we breathe or the sun which gives us light and life. Yet I believe that if no other political result than this could to-day be pointed out as coming from the colonization of America by Englishmen, we should still be justified in regarding that event as one of the most important in the history of mankind. For obviously the principle of federalism, as thus broadly stated, contains within itself the seeds of permanent peace between nations; and to this glorious end I believe it will come in the fulness of time.

And now we may begin to see distinctly what it was that the American government fought for in the late civil war,--a point which at the time was by no means clearly apprehended outside the United States. We used to hear it often said, while that war was going on, that we were fighting not so much for the emancipation of the negro as for the maintenance of our federal union; and I well remember that to many who were burning to see our country purged of the folly and iniquity of negro slavery this used to seem like taking a low and unrighteous view of the case. From the stand-point of universal history it was nevertheless the correct and proper view. The emancipation of the negro, as an incidental result of the struggle, was a priceless gain which was greeted warmly by all right-minded people. But deeper down than this question, far more subtly interwoven with the innermost fibres of our national well-being, far heavier laden too with weighty consequences for the future weal of all mankind, was the question whether this great pacific principle of union joined with independence should be overthrown by the first deep-seated social difficulty it had to encounter, or should stand as an example of priceless value to other ages and to other lands. The solution was well worth the effort it cost. There have been many useless wars, but this was not one of them, for more than most wars that have been, it was fought in the direct interest of peace, and the victory so dearly purchased and so humanely used was an earnest of future peace and happiness for the world.

The object, therefore, for which the American government fought, was the perpetual maintenance of that peculiar state of things which the federal union had created,--a state of things in which, throughout the whole vast territory over which the Union holds sway, questions between states, like questions between individuals, must be settled by legal argument and judicial decisions and not by wager of battle. Far better to demonstrate this point once for all, at whatever cost, than to be burdened hereafter, like the states of Europe, with frontier fortresses and standing armies and all the barbaric apparatus of mutual suspicion! For so great an end did this most pacific people engage in an obstinate war, and never did any war so thoroughly illustrate how military power may be wielded, when necessary, by a people that has passed entirely from the military into the industrial stage of civilization. The events falsified all the predictions that were drawn from the contemplation of societies less advanced politically. It was thought that so peaceful a people could not raise a great army on demand; yet within a twelvemonth the government had raised five hundred thousand men by voluntary enlistment. It was thought that a territory involving military operations at points as far apart as Paris and Moscow could never be thoroughly conquered; yet in April 1865 the federal armies might have inarched from end to end of the Gulf States without meeting any force to oppose them. It was thought that the maintenance of a great army would beget a military temper in the Americans and lead to manifestations of Bonapartism,--domestic usurpation and foreign aggression; yet the moment the work was done the great army vanished, and a force of twenty-five thousand men was found sufficient for the military needs of the whole country. It was thought that eleven states which had struggled so hard to escape from the federal tie could not be re-admitted to voluntary co-operation in the general government, but must henceforth be held as conquered territory,--a most dangerous experiment for any free people to try. Yet within a dozen years we find the old federal relations resumed in all their completeness, and the disunion party powerless and discredited in the very states where once it had wrought such mischief. Nay more, we even see a curiously disputed presidential election, in which the votes of the southern states were given almost with unanimity to one of the candidates, decided quietly by a court of arbitration; and we see a universal acquiescence in the decision, even in spite of a general belief that an extraordinary combination of legal subtleties resulted in adjudging the presidency to the candidate who was not really elected.

Such has been the result of the first great attempt to break up the federal union in America. It is not probable that another attempt can ever be made with anything like an equal chance of success. Here were eleven states, geographically contiguous, governed by groups of men who for half a century had pursued a well-defined policy in common, united among themselves and marked off from most of the other states by a difference far more deeply rooted in the groundwork of society than any mere economic difference,--the difference between slave-labour and free-labour. These eleven states, moreover, held such an economic relationship with England that they counted upon compelling the naval power of England to be used in their behalf. And finally it had not yet been demonstrated that the maintenance of the federal union was something for which the great mass of the people would cheerfully fight. Never could the experiment of secession be tried, apparently, under fairer auspices; yet how tremendous the defeat! It was a defeat that wrought conviction,--the conviction that no matter how grave the political questions that may arise hereafter, they must be settled in accordance with the legal methods the Constitution has provided, and that no state can be allowed to break the peace. It is the thoroughness of this conviction that has so greatly facilitated the reinstatement of the revolted states in their old federal relations; and the good sense and good faith with which the southern people, in spite of the chagrin of defeat, have accepted the situation and acted upon it, is something unprecedented in history, and calls for the warmest sympathy and admiration on the part of their brethren of the north. The federal principle in America has passed through this fearful ordeal and come out stronger than ever; and we trust it will not again be put to so severe a test. But with this principle unimpaired, there is no reason why any further increase of territory or of population should overtask the resources of our government.

In the United States of America a century hence we shall therefore doubtless have a political aggregation immeasurably surpassing in power and in dimensions any empire that has as yet existed. But we must now consider for a moment the probable future career of the English race in other parts of the world. The colonization of North America by Englishmen had its direct effects upon the eastern as well as upon the western side of the Atlantic. The immense growth of the commercial and naval strength of England between the time of Cromwell and the time of the elder Pitt was intimately connected with the colonization of North America and the establishment of plantations in the West Indies. These circumstances reacted powerfully upon the material development of England, multiplying manifold the dimensions of her foreign trade, increasing proportionately her commercial marine, and giving her in the eighteenth century the dominion over the seas. Endowed with this maritime supremacy, she has with an unerring instinct proceeded to seize upon the keys of empire in all parts of the world,--Gibraltar, Malta, the isthmus of Suez, Aden, Ceylon, the coasts of Australia, island after island in the Pacific,--every station, in short, that commands the pathways of maritime commerce, or guards the approaches to the barbarous countries which she is beginning to regard as in some way her natural heritage. Any well-filled album of postage-stamps is an eloquent commentary on this maritime supremacy of England. It is enough to turn one's head to look over her colonial blue-books. The natural outcome of all this overflowing vitality it is not difficult to foresee. No one can carefully watch what is going on in Africa to-day without recognizing it as the same sort of thing which was going on in North America in the seventeenth century; and it cannot fail to bring forth similar results in course of time. Here is a vast country, rich in beautiful scenery and in resources of timber and minerals, with a salubrious climate and fertile soil, with great navigable rivers and inland lakes, which will not much longer be left in control of tawny lions and long-eared elephants and negro fetich-worshippers. Already five flourishing English states have been established in the south, besides the settlements on the Gold Coast and those at Aden commanding the Red Sea. English explorers work their way, with infinite hardship, through its untravelled wilds, and track the courses of the Congo and the Nile as their forefathers tracked the Potomac and the Hudson.

The work of La Salle and Smith is finding its counterpart in the labours of Baker and Livingstone. Who can doubt that within two or three centuries the African continent will be occupied by a mighty nation of English descent, and covered with populous cities and flourishing farms, with railroads and telegraphs and other devices of civilization as yet undreamed of?

If we look next to Australia, we find a country of more than two-thirds the area of the United States, with a temperate climate and immense resources, agricultural and mineral,--a country sparsely peopled by a race of irredeemable savages hardly above the level of brutes. Here England within the present century has planted six greatly thriving states, concerning which I have not time to say much, but one fact will serve as a specimen. When in America we wish to illustrate in one word the wonderful growth of our so-called north-western states, we refer to Chicago,--a city of half-a-million inhabitants standing on a spot which fifty years ago was an uninhabited marsh. In Australia the city of Melbourne was founded in 1837, the year when the present queen of England began to reign, and the state of which it is the capital was hence called Victoria. This city, now[16] just forty-three years old, has a population half as great as that of Chicago, has a public library of 200,000 volumes, and has a university with at least one professor of world-wide renown. When we see, by the way, within a period of five years and at such remote points upon the earth's surface, such erudite and ponderous works in the English language issuing from the press as those of Professor Hearn of Melbourne, of Bishop Colenso of Natal, and of Mr. Hubert Bancroft of San Francisco,--even such a little commonplace fact as this is fraught with wonderful significance when we think of all that it implies. Then there is New Zealand, with its climate of perpetual spring, where the English race is now multiplying faster than anywhere else in the world unless it be in Texas and Minnesota. And there are in the Pacific Ocean many rich and fertile spots where we shall very soon see the same things going on.

It is not necessary to dwell upon such considerations as these. It is enough to point to the general conclusion, that the work which the English race began when it colonized North America is destined to go on until every land on the earth's surface that is not already the seat of an old civilization shall become English in its language, in its political habits and traditions, and to a predominant extent in the blood of its people. The day is at hand when, four-fifths of the human race will trace its pedigree to English forefathers, as four-fifths of the white people in the United States trace their pedigree to-day. The race thus spread over both hemispheres, and from the rising to the setting sun, will not fail to keep that sovereignty of the sea and that commercial supremacy which it began to acquire when England first stretched its arm across the Atlantic to the shores of Virginia and Massachusetts. The language spoken by these great communities will not be sundered into dialects like the language of the ancient Romans, but perpetual intercommunication and the universal habit of reading and writing will preserve its integrity; and the world's business will be transacted by English-speaking people to so great an extent, that whatever language any man may have learned in his infancy he will find it necessary sooner or later to learn to express his thoughts in English. And in this way it is by no means improbable that, as Grimm the German and Candolle the Frenchman long since foretold, the language of Shakespeare may ultimately become the language of mankind.

In view of these considerations as to the stupendous future of the English race, does it not seem very probable that in due course of time Europe--which has learned some valuable lessons from America already--will find it worth while to adopt the lesson of federalism? Probably the European states, in order to preserve their relative weight in the general polity of the world, will find it necessary to do so. In that most critical period of American history between the winning of independence and the framing of the Constitution, one of the strongest of the motives which led the confederated states to sacrifice part of their sovereignty by entering into a federal union was their keen sense of their weakness when taken severally. In physical strength such a state as Massachusetts at that time amounted to little more than Hamburg or Bremen; but the thirteen states taken together made a nation of respectable power. Even the wonderful progress we have made in a century has not essentially changed this relation of things. Our greatest state, New

York, taken singly, is about the equivalent of Belgium; our weakest state, Nevada, would scarcely be a match for tha county of Dorset; yet the United States, taken together, are probably at this moment the strongest nation in the world.

Now a century hence, with a population of six hundred millions in the United States, and a hundred and fifty millions in Australia and New Zealand, to say nothing of the increase of power in other parts of the English-speaking world, the relative weights will be very different from what they were in 1788. The population of Europe will not increase in anything like the same proportion, and a very considerable part of the increase will be transferred by emigration to the English-speaking world outside of Europe. By the end of the twentieth century such nations as France and Germany can only claim such a relative position in the political world as Holland and Switzerland now occupy. Their greatness in thought and scholarship, in industrial and aesthetic art, will doubtless continue unabated. But their political weights will severally have come to be insignificant; and as we now look back, with historic curiosity, to the days when Holland was navally and commercially the rival of England, so people will then need to be reminded that there was actually once a time when little France was the most powerful nation on the earth. It will then become as desirable for the states of Europe to enter into a federal union as it was for the states of North America a century ago.

It is only by thus adopting the lesson of federalism that Europe can do away with the chances of useless warfare which remain so long as its different states own no allegiance to any common authority. War, as we have seen, is with barbarous races both a necessity and a favourite occupation. As long as civilization comes into contact with barbarism, it remains a too frequent necessity. But as between civilized and Christian nations it is a wretched absurdity. One sympathizes keenly with wars such as that which Russia has lately concluded, for setting free a kindred race endowed with capacity for progress, and for humbling the worthless barbarian who during four centuries has wrought such incalculable damage to the European world. But a sanguinary struggle for the Rhine frontier, between two civilized Christian nations who have each enough work to do in ithe world without engaging in such a strife as this, will, I am sure, be by and by condemned by the general opinion of mankind. Such questions will have to be settled by discussion in some sort of federal council or parliament, if Europe would keep pace with America in the advance towards universal law and order. All will admit that such a state of things is a great desideratum: let us see if it is really quite so utopian as it may seem at the first glance. No doubt the lord who dwelt in Haddon Hall in the fifteenth century would have thought it very absurd if you had told him that within four hundred years it would not be necessary for country gentlemen to live in great stone dungeons with little cross-barred windows and loopholes from which to shoot at people going by. Yet to-day a country gentleman in some parts of Massachusetts may sleep securely without locking his front-door. We have not yet done away with robbery and murder, but we have at least made private warfare illegal; we have arrayed public opinion against it to such an extent that the police-court usually makes short shrift for the misguided man who tries to wreak vengeance on his enemy. Is it too much to hope that by and by we may similarly put public warfare under the ban? I think not. Already in America, as wre have seen, it has become customary to deal with questions between states just as we would deal with questions between individuals. This we have seen to be the real purport of American federalism. To have established such a system ovrer one great continent is to have made a very good beginning towards establishing it over the world. To establish such a system in Europe will no doubt be difficult, for here we have to deal with an immense complication of prejudices, intensified by linguistic and ethnological differences. Nevertheless the pacific pressure exerted upon Europe by America is becoming so great that it will doubtless before long overcome all these obstacles. I refer to the industrial competition between the old and the new worlds, which has become so conspicuous within the last ten years. Agriculturally Minnesota, Nebraska, and Kansas are already formidable competitors with England, France, and Germany; but this is but the beginning. It is but the first spray from the tremendous wave of economic competition that is gathering in the Mississippi valley. By and by, when our shameful tariff--falsely called "protective"--shall have been done away with, and our manufacturers shall produce superior articles at less cost of raw material, we shall begin to compete with European countries in all the markets of the world; and the competition in manufactures will become as keen as it is now beginning to be in agriculture. This time will not be long in coming, for our tariff-system has already begun to be discussed, and in the light of our present knowledge discussion means its doom. Born of crass ignorance and self-defeating greed, it cannot bear the light. When this curse to American labour--scarcely less blighting than the; curse of negro slavery--shall have been once removed, the economic pressure exerted upon Europe by the United States will soon become very great indeed. It will not be long before this economic pressure will make it simply impossible for the states of Europe to keep up such military armaments as they are now maintaining. The disparity between the United States, with a standing army of only twenty-five thousand men withdrawn from industrial pursuits, and the states of Europe, with their standing armies amounting to four millions of men, is something that cannot possibly be kept up. The economic competition will become so keen that European armies will have to be disbanded, the swords will have to be turned into ploughshares, and thus the victory of the industrial over the military type of civilization will at last become complete. But to disband the great armies of Europe will necessarily involve the forcing of the great states of Europe into some sort of federal relation, in which Congresses--already held on rare occasions--will become more frequent, in which the principles of international law will acquire a more definite sanction, and in which the combined physical power of all the states will constitute (as it now does in America) a permanent threat against any state that dares to wish for selfish reasons to break the peace. In some such way as this, I believe, the industrial development of the English race outside of Europe will by and by enforce federalism upon Europe. As regards the serious difficulties that grow out of prejudices attendant upon differences in language, race, and creed, a most valuable lesson is furnished us by the history of Switzerland. I am inclined to think that the greatest contribution which Switzerland has made to the general progress of civilization has been to show us how such obstacles can be surmounted, even on a small scale. To surmount them on a great scale will soon become the political problem of Europe; and it is America which has set the example and indicated the method.

Thus we may foresee in general outline how, through the gradual concentration of the preponderance of physical power into the hands of the most pacific communities, the wretched business of warfare must finally become obsolete all over the globe. The element of distance is now fast becoming eliminated from political problems, and the history of human progress politically will continue in the future to be what it has been in the past,--the history of the successive union of groups of men into larger and more complex aggregates. As this process goes on, it may after many more ages of political experience become apparent that there is really no reason, in the nature of things, why the whole of mankind should not constitute politically one huge federation,--each little group managing its local affairs in entire independence, but relegating all questions of international interest to the decision of one central tribunal supported by the public opinion of the entire human race. I believe that the time will come when such a state of things will exist upon the earth, when it will be possible (with our friends of the Paris dinner-party) to speak of the UNITED STATES as stretching from pole to pole,--or, with Tennyson, to celebrate the "parliament of man and the federation of the world." Indeed, only when such a state of things has begun to be realized, can Civilization, as sharply demarcated from Barbarism, be said to have fairly begun. Only then can the world be said to have become truly Christian. Many ages of toil and doubt and perplexity will no doubt pass by before such a desideratum is reached. Meanwhile it is pleasant to feel that the dispassionate contemplation of great masses of historical facts goes far towards confirming our faith in this ultimate triumph of good over evil. Our survey began with pictures of horrid slaughter and desolation: it ends with the picture of a world covered with cheerful homesteads, blessed with a sabbath of perpetual peace.

[Footnote 1: Freeman, "Norman Conquest," v. 482.]

[Footnote 2: Freeman, "Comparative Politics," 264.]

[Footnote 3: This is disputed, however. See Ross, "Early History of Landholding among the Germans."]

[Footnote 4: Stubbs, "Constitutional History," i. 84.]

[Footnote 5: Kemble, "Saxons in England," i. 59.]

[Footnote 6: Maine, "Village Communities," Lond., 1871, p. 132.]

[Footnote 7: Stubbs, "Constitutional History," i. 85.]

[Footnote 8: Freeman, "Comparative Politics," 118.]

[Footnote 9: Geffroy, "Rome et les Barbares," 209.]

[Footnote 10: Maine, "Village Communities," 118.]

[Footnote 11: Stubbs, "Constitutional History," i. 625.]

[Footnote 12: Stubbs, "Select Charters," 401.]

[Footnote 13: "La Cit?Antique," 441.]

[Footnote 14: Arnold, "Roman Provincial Administration," 237.]

[Footnote 15: Stubbs, "Select Charters," 401.]

[Footnote 16: In 1880.]

INDEX.

Nelson's statue in Trafalgar Square, Nevada, New England confederacy, New York, New Zealand, Norman conquest, North America, struggle for possession of,

Omar,

Pagus, Paris, American dinner-party in, Parish, its relation to township, Parkman, F. Pax romana Peace of the world, how secured, Peerage of England Peloponnesian war Persian war against Greece Pestilences Petersham Philip, King Phratries Pictet, A. Poland Pontiac Population of United States a century hence Private property in land Problem of political civilization Protestantism and Catholicism, political question at stake between Prussia conquered by Teutonic knights Puritanism Puritans of New England, their origin

Quebec, Wolfe's victory at

Rebellion against Charles I. Redivision of arable lands Re-election of town officers Representation unknown to Greeks and Romans origin of federal, in United States Rex Rhode Island Roman law Rome, plebeian revolution at early stages of secret of its power advantages of its dominion causes of its political failure, powerful influence of, in Middle Ages meaning of its great wars Roses, wars of the Ross, D. Russia, Mongolian conquest of village communities in its late war against the Turks its despotic government contrasted with that of France under Old Regime

SARACENS Scandinavia Secession, war of Selectmen Self-government preserved in England lost in France Shakespeare Shires Shottery, cottage at Smith, J. Social war South Carolina Spain, Roman conquest of Sparta State sovereignty in America Strasburg Strategic position of England Stubbs, W. Suez Swiss cantonal assemblies Switzerland, lesson of its history self-government preserved in

Tacitus Tariff in America Tax-taking despotisms Tennyson, A. Teutonic civilization contrasted with Graeco-Roman Teutonic knights Teutonic village

THE END.

www.ingramcontent.com/pod-product-compliance
Lightning Source LLC
Chambersburg PA
CBHW070400290526
45790CB00004B/1575